BLIZZARD '79

A Survivor's Souvenir and Scrapbook

BLIZZARD '79

A Survivor's Souvenir and Scrapbook
By the Staff of The Chicago Sun-Times

Zay N. Smith, Editor

Maury Falstein, Picture Editor

Features Press, Indianapolis, Indiana 46220

BLIZZARD '79

A Survivor's Souvenir and Scrapbook

Introduction

The weather forecasters were optimistic. Chicago had just suffered through its coldest winter in history (1977) and its snowiest (1978). Such brutal winters rarely came in threes.

The psychics agreed. The winter of 1979 would be "20 percent less severe than last winter," one said. Another foresaw high winds as the only problem.

But the new winter hit early, and it hit hard.

The steady snowfalls of November and December gave the first warning. It was noticed, even then, that the snow was piling up faster than it had during the previous record year.

A violent winter storm—ten inches of fresh snow with high winds and deep drifts—next arrived to surprise revelers on New Year's Eve. The city staggered. Thousands were stranded.

A record cold wave followed. For ten days, while the city and suburbs struggled to dig out, the thermometer stayed at zero or below.

And then came the Blizzard of '79.

The record keepers have noted that after the January 12-14 blizzard, Chicago had twenty-nine inches of snow on the ground—the most the city had ever seen at any one miserable moment. They have noted, too, that the all-time record for total snowfall—82.3 inches, nearly seven feet—was broken on February 12, with at least a month of winter weather to go.

But most Chicagoans will simply note, and long remember, what it was like to live in a city that had become the world's largest snow sculpture: all the weeks of coping with collapsed roofs, closed airports, disappearing boulevards, buried automobiles and trains that never came.

That much for starters.

This is a survivor's souvenir of the winter that took Chicago by storm. The story is told by Chicago *Sun-Times* reporters, columnists, photographers and artists.

Sun-Times special writer Paul Galloway recalls the Blizzard of '79 in detail. M. W. Newman compares it with the one that mugged the city in 1967. Reporter William Braden, with plenty of evidence surrounding him, takes a new new look at the theory that no two snowflakes are alike.

Columnist Mike Royko reports on the Chicago-style political story that snowballed in the great storm's aftermath. "In no other city," he writes, "would a record snowfall eventually be revealed to have a crime syndicate connection."

Columnist Roger Simon reveals some startling solutions to the city's snow crisis—by way of the Mayor's Office of Blocked Streets, Frozen Roads and Total Confusion—and reports on the Chicago City Council's unique theological approach.

More than a hundred photographs show how hard the Chicago area was hit—and how hard it fought back.

Among other highlights: items from Kup's Column and Bob Herguth's Public Eye, and selected cartoons by Jacob Burck, John Fischetti and Bill Mauldin.

There is a scrapbook section in the back where survivors can paste their own snapshots and recollections.

—Zay N. Smith

Contents

The Cold Before the Storm

Friday: Warmer

Forecast for Chicago Area

Cloudy and warmer with a 90 percent chance of occasional snow. High in the mid teens; low 5 to 10. East to southeasterly winds 12 to 20 m.p.h. Cloudy and cold Saturday with a chance of snow; high in the middle or upper teens.

Midwest Weather Forecast

A travelers' advisory has been issued for Illinois, Indiana, and western and southern Wisconsin in the morning. Snow accumulations of 2 to 4 inches are likely in northern and central Illinois, southern and western Wisconsin and northwest Indiana. 1 to 3 inches possible in southeastern Indiana and southern Illinois. Periods of snow will continue throughout the region during the day and diminish from the north Friday night.

Extended Outlook

(Sunday through Tuesday): Very cold Sunday with fair skies. Highs 5 to 13 north and 13 to 23 south; lows 2 below to 12 below north and 2 below to 11 above south. Not so cold Monday and Tuesday with a chance of snow north on Monday and over the state on Tuesday. Highs from the lower to middle 20's north and middle 20's to upper 30's south; lows 5 to 20 north and 10 to 30 south.

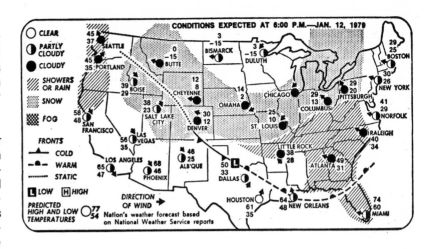

Saturday: Snow

Forecast for Chicago Area

Snow to continue with accumulations of 2 to 4 inches by afternoon. High in the middle or upper 20's; low around 10 near the lake to zero in the far western sections. Northeasterly winds 15 to 25 m.p.h. Partly cloudy and colder Sunday with a high 10 to 15.

Midwest Weather Forecast

Cloudy throughout the region with snow accumulating 4 inches or more in central Illinois, 2 to 4 inches in northern Illinois and southern Wisconsin and 1 to 2 inches elsewhere. Highs from around 5 to the teens northwest, the 20's central and the 30's southeast; overnight lows from 25 below in extreme northwest sections, zero to 10 below central and the teens to 20's southeast. Sunday will see sunny skies northwest, partly sunny in central areas and cloudy with snow diminishing to flurries in the southeast. Highs from 5 below to 10 above northwest to the teens and 20's southeast.

Extended Outlook

(Monday through Wednesday): Very cold; chance of snow in the south sections on Monday and over the state on Tuesday. Highs 3 to 18 north and 15 to 32 south; lows 12 below zero to 5 above north and zero to 15 above south.

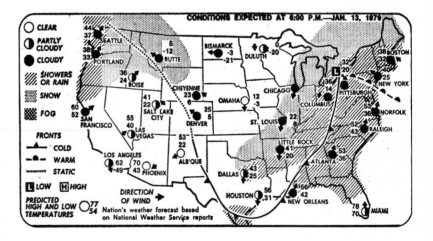

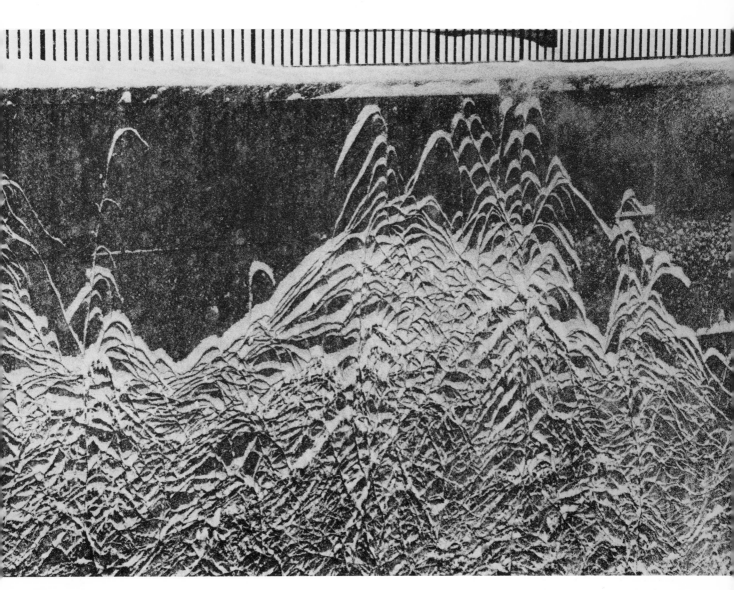

*Snow-edged vines clinging to the side
of the IBM Building above the Chicago River
at State Street.*

It Snowed, and It Snowed, and It Snowed

(above left) A tow truck pulls a driver out of a snow bank at the westbound exit to the Ryan from I-55.
(left) A car spins out of control on the Dan Ryan Expressway. (below) Car buried in a four-foot pile of drifted snow.

No two snowflakes alike? Go ahead, prove it!

"How do they really know?" asked the disembodied voice in the dark bedroom.

I pried one eye open. The red glow of the digital clock informed me it was one in the morning.

"How does who really know what, Beatrice?"

"Those scientists who write about snowflakes. They always say it—that no two snowflakes are alike. How do they know that?"

"I don't know," I said.

"Find out," she said.

Digging my way out of the driveway next morning, I wondered how many snowflakes were in each of the several hundred shovelfuls I heaved on the growing mounds that now towered above my head. Hundreds of thousands? Millions? How could they possibly all be the same?

Driving to work in a world of white, I felt a mounting hatred of all those damnable Identified Flying Objects. Somehow, the thought that each of them was different made that hatred all the more intense. It wasn't rational. But who in Chicago is rational these days?

When I arrived at work at The Sun-Times, I went to the newspaper's library and asked for the S volume of the World Book Encyclopedia. Maybe the experts had changed their minds. Or maybe they had at least stopped making that infuriating statement.

The 1979 edition of the encyclopedia had just arrived. I opened the volume to the article titled SNOW and read:

"Snow always appears as tiny, six-sided crystals. But no two snow crystals are exactly alike."

Curses!

I phoned the World Book and asked where I could find George F. Taylor, the author of the article. I learned he is a highly respected geologist, meteorologist and former manager of scientific computing at the Lockheed Missiles & Space Co. I phoned him at his home in Menlo Park, California, and asked if he had in fact written that article, and if he had in fact made that statement, and he confessed that he had. I paused, savoring the moment, and then I asked him, through clenched teeth:

"How do you *know* none of them are exactly alike?"

"Well", he said, "we haven't looked at all of them, certainly. I imagine if you looked far enough you could probably find a couple . . ."

"A couple exactly alike? You're prepared to *admit* that?"

"Well, unless you've looked at an awful lot of them, I guess you can't say for sure that no two are alike. But that's what the people who have really studied them say. Some of the people who've studied snowflakes in detail have looked at thousands of them, and on the basis of their sample they say that. But of course there are millions of flakes in just a small snowstorm, so nobody can really say we'll never find two alike. But, in general — hah! hah! — they all look different."

"But why do the snowflake people say that if they don't really know?"

"Oh, I don't think it's a very objective statement to make. I think the real reason for a statement like that is, if you don't look at it that way, you might think, well, a snowflake is a snowflake is a snowflake; they're all the same. So, I think the purpose of that statement was to point out they are very different. When you look at hundreds of them or thousands of them, they all appear to be different. But I'm sure nobody set out to prove that they were. Nobody's tried to quantify their differences, because nobody thought that was very important. They're not like a biological species where you can say that something's different from something or other and give real reasons."

"Would it be fair to say there is no sound, objective, scientific data to substantiate that statement?"

"Oh, I don't think there is. I really don't."

"The statement sort of perpetuates itself?"

"Well, yeah."

"So you think if I really put my mind to it, I could find two identical snowflakes?"

"I'm sure you could. There's nothing about their production to indicate they have to be so different. It just appears that they are."

Taylor agreed that the incredible number of snowflakes would virtually ensure the production of twins. Since he was being such a nice guy about it, I asked him if he'd come up with a number. For example, could he estimate how many snowflakes were in the twenty-odd inches that fell on Chicago during the first phase of the Blizzard of '79?

He didn't have his calculator with him, but he started mumbling a series of numbers and conversions. Then he said:

"Just taking the area within the city limits, and doing it in my head, I'd say a fair number would be twenty-five times ten to the thirteenth power snowflakes for that particular storm. That's twenty-five followed by thirteen zeros. Or, to make that more familiar, you could express it as 250 trillion.

"That's quite a few snowflakes. You could compare it with the number of stars in our Milky Way galaxy, which is about 100 billion. And we're talking about 2,500 times more snowflakes than stars in this case, which is just a very rough guesstimate, of course. And you might want to check those figures. I might have missed a power of ten somewhere."

Again, that 250 trillion is just for twenty inches that fell in the city—not counting the suburbs. And total snowfall this winter is already seventy-three inches. Just in the Chicago area. And twenty-three percent of the Earth, or forty-eight million square miles, is permanently or temporarily covered with snow.

I rushed home that night with the good news.

"You were right, Beatrice! They don't really know. In fact, it's not even true!"

And with a sigh of peace and relief, I snuggled down under the covers that night for a long winter's nap.

Until the voice came in the darkness.

"Fingerprints . . ."

—William Braden

(left) Pedestrian at Wacker and South Water Streets. (right) Southbound JFK traffic from Augusta Boulevard. (below) Commuters trudging across Wacker Drive at Madison.

Sideviews — Paul Galloway

On the day it struck, Chicago awoke complacent and unsuspecting, like a rube from the sticks whistling as he walked through a big-city high-crime area. The mugging would come soon enough.

John Wayne's operation was on Page 1. The National Weather Service forecast, tucked innocently inside the newspapers, said that two to four inches of snow was expected by afternoon, when a new cold spell would arrive, snuff out the snow and merely make us miserable.

The city announced that Operation Snow-Tow, which was still clearing the nine to ten inches of dreck from the New Year's Eve blizzard off the streets, would be suspended until Monday because of heavy weekend evening travel.

Heh, heh.

The Great Storm, a monster out of Mother Nature by Old Man Winter, stomped in and stayed.

On Saturday, January 13, a date that invites superstition, the statistics are spectacular. From midnight to 6 a.m., 3.7 inches fell. In the next six hours, 5.8 inches piled up. From noon to midnight, seven more inches of the stuff parachuted in.

The grand total, from January 12-14, is 20.3 inches. Press that figure in your book of memories. Though it's a strong second to the twenty-three inches that fell in the Big Snow of '67, the nine inches already on the ground, gave us twenty-nine inches. A record for Chicago! Hurrah! Yeeecccch!

Skiier bogs down in the knee-deep snow at the lakefront.

Sideviews

Out of the bosom of the Air,
Out of the cloud-folds of her garments shaken,
Over the woodlands brown and bare
Over the harvest-fields forsaken,
Silent, and soft, and slow
Descends the snow.

—Henry Wadsworth Longfellow
"Snowflakes"

Ahhhh, shut up.

More snow facts: Snowflakes are hexagonal and, just as you've always heard, no two are alike. The German word for snow is *schnee*, Latin is *nix*, French is *neige* and Russian *sneg*. The Eskimos, who are authorities, have two words, *qanit* for falling and *aput* for lying snow. Snow, permanently or temporarily, covers twenty-three percent of Earth.

Snow is a synonym for cocaine in the drug-users' jargon.

A gang of snowplows heads south on Lake Shore Drive.

Sideviews

The 1967 storm lasted thirty-six hours. The 1979 storm lasted thirty-nine hours.

The Morning After Was a Big Snow Job

"I'll take three people," said one generous motorist to a huddled mass of shivering people waiting for a warm bus on N. Sheridan Rd.

Almost immediately he was swamped with people hoping for a seat out of the bitter winds.

The scene was repeated all over the city as the hammer fell on one of the worst winter mornings Chicago had seen—record-setting low temperatures accompanying record accumulations of snow.

It was so bad that the National Weather Service couldn't even keep accurate records. On Sunday, forecasters said there were twenty-nine inches of the snow on the ground; on Monday, the figure was twenty-six inches.

"Yeah, three inches blew away," one forecaster said.

"Where?" a reporter asked.

"Oh, it blew from the spot where we are measuring it at Midway [Airport]," he said.

The statistician's salve was little comfort to the rest of us.

Even the U.S. Postal Service had its problems—neither rain nor sleet nor ridiculous conspiracy of the elements aside.

At the Irving Park postal station, 3319 N. Cicero, only about thirty-five of sixty-five letter-carriers made it to work, and only about a third of the inside clerks made it.

"I guess some people just won't get their mail," said one supervisor, who asked that his name not be used. "We'll make all the business deliveries, though. With O'Hare closed, we haven't gotten much mail, but we won't be able to deliver it all anyway."

What about the post office's unrelenting image?

"Just compare it to the big snow of '67, then I'm sure the people will understand," the supervisor said.

Some people just loved the weather, however—especially those who could make a buck.

Curtis Barron, of People's AMC, 2223 N. Cicero, said, "I'm enjoying the weather half to death.

"Oh, my God, sales of Jeeps and four-wheel-drive cars have been unbelievable, just amazing. We're cleared out except for nine or ten jeeps. People come in here and say, 'I wanta take it home, now.'

"Over the weekend, we sold thirty Jeeps. Normally, we sell two or three. Maybe we'd have sold more cars, instead, but nobody wants 'em."

How bad was business on the day after? Manager Elvis Williams of the North Loop garage, 70 W. Lake, said, "Nobody's coming downtown today." He estimated that Monday's activity was "ten percent of normal."

For more reliable information, we asked the Chicago Association of Commerce and Industry what percentages of businesses were operating Monday.

"I can't tell you," was the response. "Our research department wasn't able to get in today."

About eighteen kidney dialysis patients made it to Roosevelt Hospital, 426 W. Wisconsin, for their treatments. Because medical vehicles couldn't get through the snow-clogged streets, some arrived on chair stretchers.

"All our other [out-patient] clinics are closed," said Linda Bailey, director of social services for the hospital, "but dialysis has to go on."

For some people, it was a miracle to simply get to work.

"When I went to the 87th St. Dan Ryan station," one woman recounted, "there was a sign in the cashier's booth which said 'You'd be better off on the bus'."

The sign was entirely accurate, since the Lake-Dan Ryan train that followed was unable to negotiate the incline just past the Cermak Rd. station in two attempts.

After an hour's wait in an unheated train, "they finally brought up another train which gave us a push from behind. It was quite a push; the whole train shuddered as we were knocked by the other train." The trip to Adams and Wabash mercifully ended two hours after it had started.

Transportation was easier at the Brookfield Zoo where, according to spokeswoman Joyce Gardella, Clydesdale horses were being used to deliver food around the 204-acre park.

"Our snow-moving equipment got stalled, so we just used the horses," Gardella said. "They cut through the drifts as if they were butter. The Clydesdales will get through where other things don't." She said the Siberian tigers and snow leopards were having a "marvelous time."

Not quite the case at the Dirksen Federal Building, 219 S. Dearborn, where justice was delayed by the weather and by the now-infamous heating system, which went on the blink about 8:30 a.m. Monday.

Heavy sweaters and jackets were the order of the day for the few lawyers and judges who made it to work. Indoor temperatures never got far above the fifties, and one trial, before U.S. District Court Judge Frank J. McGarr, was continued when only nine of the fourteen jurors and alternates appeared in court.

At 3 p.m., the final order came from Chief Judge James B. Parsons. He ruled it was in order for everybody to go home.

But by late Monday afternoon, new layers of snow were falling. One bus driver, who kept encountering stalled cars on his 155 route on Devon Av., enlisted a group of enthusiastic teenagers to help out. "They would all jump out and push stalled cars," one non-participant said, "then jump back in the bus so they could keep moving."

There would be no snow on one spot, however. In front of City Hall, one passerby watched as six members of the city sewer department smashed ice, shoveled snow and spread salt for almost half an hour on a forty-foot section of sidewalk.

"If the city spent as much time cleaning up the other streets as it did on the one sidewalk," he complained, "snow removal would take twenty to forty years."

Oh well. At least there was a sidewalk that worked.

—Michael Zielenziger

(above) Janssen Street between Grace and Byron buried in three- to four-foot drifts. (above right) This woman cleared off her windshield, but had nowhere to go at Mohawk just north of North. (right) Snow-covered Elk Grove.

(above) This gas station just south of Roosevelt Road on Route 59 is completely snowed in. (below) Heads of parking meters poke above the drifts in parking lot to the south of the Planetarium. (right) A cab driver sends up clouds of steam and exhaust as he tries to extricate himself from the Randolph exit ramp on the Kennedy Expressway.

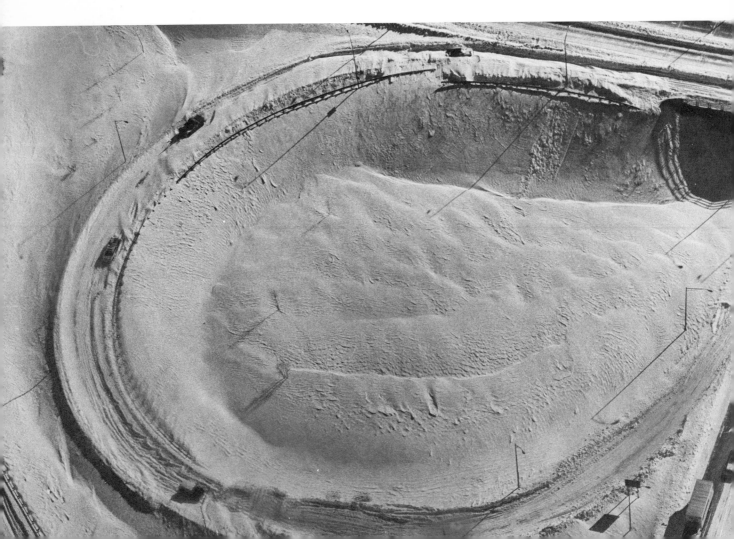

(left) Snow-covered car in the middle of St. Paul Street at North Park. (below left) Four autos are stranded on a cloverleaf ramp connecting the Northwest Tollway with Route 53 near the Woodfield Shopping Center. (below) Intersection of Palatine Road and Arlington Heights Road.

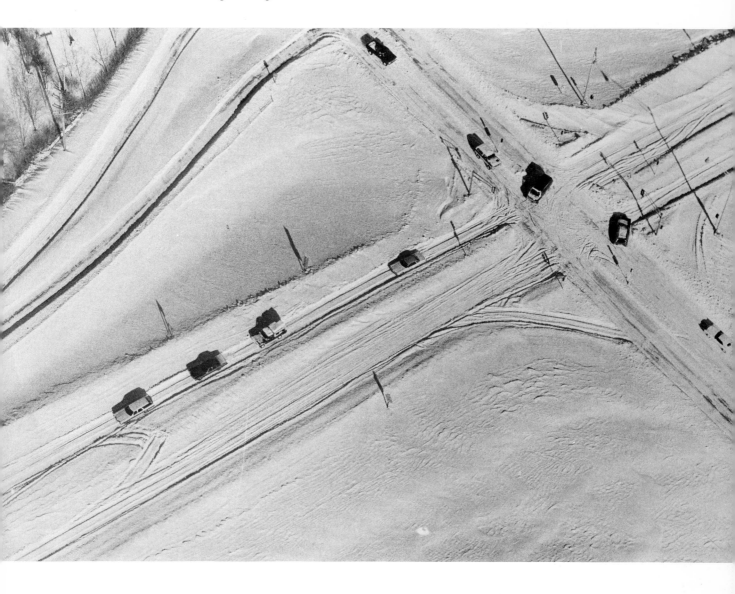

"I Tried To Get Out . . ."

(above) A snowbound motorist near North and Clark warms
up inside his auto while his shovel sits in the snowbank.
(right) Looking east on Altgeld from Greenview.

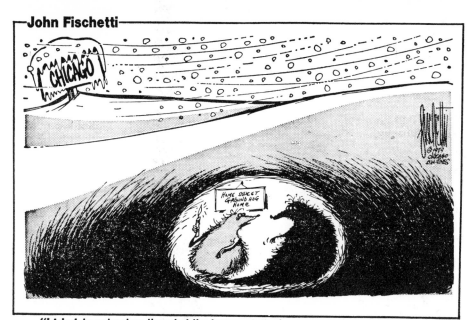

"**I tried** to get out on time, but the transportation's **completely** bogged down."

(left) Car stranded on Belden west of Halsted. (below) Digging out of the 3300 block on Wallace. (right) Cleaning Janssen Street between Grace and Byron.

(left) Snow-clogged side street on the South Side. (below) Motorist is stalled on ramp leading to I-90.

"... But the Transportation Is Completely Bogged Down."

Waiting in the Greyhound Bus Terminal at Clark and Randolph.

The 'diary' of a storm at O'Hare

How did the gargantuan O'Hare cope with the latest snow crisis? Not very well, many frustrated travelers stranded at the world's busiest airport during the Blizzard of '79 complained. Reasonably well, considering the weather conditions, airport and city officials said.

Here's a chronicle of what weather information airport officials had and how they responded:

January 12, Friday

On that day, city operations personnel who work in the O'Hare control tower knew a major snowfall was expected by the next morning, O'Hare logs show. Operations people also knew it would be dumped on top of the nine inches of unmelted snow remaining from the fourteen-inch New Year's weekend storm. Because more than one inch of snow was expected—the total would be twenty-eight inches when measured at 6 a.m. January 14—city crews started manning snow equipment, working in twelve-hour shifts, and the seven private contractors who clear the ramp areas were called.

January 13, Saturday

At 2 a.m., O'Hare logs state, three to five more inches of snow was expected in the next eighteen to twenty-four hours. Arriving and departing aircraft were using one of six runways, 14 Right. The other runways were closed because of snow, and city crews were plowing Runways 4 Right and 9 Right. Which runways to clear is determined by a snow committee of city, airlines and Federal Aviation Administration officials. Several factors, including wind conditions, affect their decision. Changing winds play a major role in determining use of runways, and even in the middle of summer, winds can limit runway use. O'Hare pioneered the snow committee concept and it has been copied at other airports around the world, FAA spokesman Neal Callahan said.

During any major snow, all components of the airport must be working for planes to arrive and depart. Roads from the expressway, the ramp area connecting to the terminal where passengers board planes, the internal roadway network, runways, taxiways, high-speed turning areas and holding pads must all be cleared of snow, and all of the snow clearing must be done at the same time, according to airport manager John Carr.

Crews must take care not to form high hills that could obstruct an aircraft or cause interference with radio signals, so the snow has to be hauled to dumps in the airport and smoothed into relatively low piles.

At 8:07 a.m. January 13, Runway 9 Right was opened for departing flights, but it was closed at 10:38 a.m. because of a disabled aircraft. Arrivals and departures were continuing on Runway 14 Right.

The poor weather caused braking conditions on 14 Right to deteriorate at 12:26 p.m., and the runway was restricted to departing flights.

At 1 p.m., with 8.7 inches of snow dumped on O'Hare—and eight to ten more expected—the airport closed. Snow removal had been proceeding on Runway 4 Right, but a predicted change in wind direction caused work to stop there and crews were sent to Runway 14 Right.

But at 10:53 p.m., visability was below one-quarter of a mile and unsafe for the giant and specialized snow-clearing machines to work on 14 Right. So, work was discontinued on that runway. Men and equipment were shifted and work continued on taxiways, ramps and gate positions.

January 14, Sunday

On that cold day, the temperature, seven degrees at 6 a.m., the airport remained closed. Mel Volz, a former chairman of the airport snow committee and United Airlines central division vice president of flight operations, said of that day: "I have never seen snow at that intensity at sixteen degrees and winds gusting to thirty-five knots. You normally do not get heavy snow with those low temperatures.

"The snow adhered to everything it touched, almost like a layer of concrete. It just kept coming and never stopped. Another problem we never experienced was the covering of runway lights and runway edge lighting," he said.

The field lights are about a foot tall and many were buried in the snow. Carr said crews first were sent to find the lights and mark each with an orange pennant. Other crews had to hand-shovel the lights out.

Complicating this was the weight of the snow, which snapped the bases of many of the lights, causing short circuits that further delayed the opening of the runways.

All this plus the liquid de-icer used, a glycol-based solution, was ineffective in temperatures below fifteen degrees. Also, the heated sand (about 400 degrees) used to cover and melt the snow cooled too quickly in the deep chill.

With the airport closed, work proceeded January 14 in clearing 14 Right, the longest runway, chosen because of predicted wind conditions.

January 15, Monday

The airport officially reopened at 6:29 a.m. with snow removal starting on Runways 27 Left and 32 Left. The temperature: minus fifteen degrees. But at 7 a.m., FAA

Stranded passengers and lost baggage at O'Hare.

records show, drifting snows covered eleven FAA instrument landing sites about 1,000 feet from the end of several runways. That day, 697 flights used the airport. The FAA asked the city for help in clearing the areas around radio antennas emitting electronic signals that guide aircraft to the runway. Snow on the ground—or any object—can dangerously distort the signal. "This was the very first time we had to clear the sites," manager Carr said.

January 16, Tuesday

Snow-plowing continued, but drifting snow meant no end to the job, and some runways had to be resanded so the planes could brake. Still, 1,085 flights arrived or departed.

With city crews working in twelve-hour shifts, by January 18, traffic was above normal, and 2,162 planes arrived and departed O'Hare Airport.

And next time? "We have a debriefing after every storm," Carr said, "on a first-name cursing basis."

Plans to do better are in the works, Carr said. Preliminary approval has already been given to raise the height of the field lights, which were buried in the snow. Key to doing better is more snow-removal equipment to add to the fifty-six pieces the city already owns. Some equipment already has been ordered and delivery is expected in the fall.

Mel Volz, the former snow committee chairman, said the airlines, which foot the bill for O'Hare, will be looking at the economic impact of the blizzard. "The impact we felt this year convinced a lot of people we can spend more money for equipment even if we don't need it every winter."

—Lynn Sweet

Snowed in at O'Hare.

Sideviews

The closing of O'Hare from Saturday to 6 a.m. Monday caused a fifty-four-hour delay for the Lyric Opera Chorus, part of a party of 107 persons trying to get to Milan, Italy, to perform the European debut of "Paradise Lost."

They could have, but didn't, pass their time singing, "Nobody Knows the Trouble I've Seen," but they did sing other selections. And when they got the good news that their flight was about to depart, they really had something to sing about. And they did.

(left) Snowed in at O'Hare. (below) Sleeping passengers awaiting take-off at O'Hare.

"South? I don't even know which way is up."

Sideviews

O'Hare Airport, which was closed for almost two full days, only the sixth time in its history, was a scene of confusion, frustration and disappointment. Some travelers took the cancellations with remarkable equanimity. But, the Wall Street Journal reported, one woman whose flight to New York was canceled made a nagging nuisance of herself. She hated the airline and she hated Chicago. When a runway finally opened, she was put on a plane just to get rid of her. The plane's destination was . . . the West Coast.

(left) Snowbound pheasants at Midway Airport.
(above) Snowplows clearing the field at
O'Hare.

ARRIVALS

FLIGHT	DUE TO ARRIVE	WILL ARRIVE	GATE	REMARKS	FLIGHT
651	10:07			CANCELLED	109
415	10:11			CANCELLED	65
235	10:20			CANCELLED	381
234	10:26			CANCELLED	364
291	10:35			CANCELLED	148
340	10:38			CANCELLED	427
105	11:05			DETROIT	293
287	11:06			CANCELLED	210
89	11:07			CANCELLED	
161	11:08			CANCELLED	231
371	11:09			CANCELLED	167
863	11:09			CANCELLED	437

AMERICAN AIRLINES

Sideviews

"People are very anxious to get out of town, but it's difficult to find space for them in hotels," said Ron Murray, a vacation counselor, something we all need, at Thomas Cook Travel, 435 N. Michigan.

"People want to go to exotic places, like a little cottage on a beach in St. Croix, or the Princess or Condessa hotels in Acapulco. Jamaica is a big request right now."

Danza DeGraff, Weston Travel in Westmont: "Every seat is filled. As far as we're concerned, the airlines have no seats going to Miami, Fort Lauderdale, Orlando or Tampa today (Friday.) We've hired another person because of the volume of calls.

"Young and old alike, people want to get out of town."

Hear! Hear!

Digging Out: City

(above) An auto is protected by snowbanks on three sides as it sits in its parking space on Armitage near Larrabee. (left) Chairs guarding cleared-out parking spaces on the 2600 block of Burling.

The Great Debate is on: is '79 worse than '67?

Has Chicago's atrocious blizzard of '79 been worse than its ferocious blitz of '67?

It's a toss-up. There have been fewer deaths this time, and less anguish—so far, at any rate. We have had more chance to mobilize and fight back—just because the big crunch began on a light working day, a Saturday.

Most of us were able to escape the worst effects and watch safely at home, on television, as the weekend deep freeze piled up.

In '67, the brute fell out of the sky during a heavy work day: Thursday, January 26. Its sixty m.p.h. gusts, enormous drifts and blinding snow stranded people and wheels all over the place, and made the trip home hellish. Five hours was about average. Just about everyone had a tale to tell.

But comparing the two killer blizzards may be about the same as trying to tell the difference between being hit on the head by a four-ton icicle or an 8,000-pound snowball.

In both cases, this metropolis of seven million was caught off guard and was crushed under tons of frozen fury. We were slammed, battered, knocked stiff by a heavyweight puncher. But, then as now, we never gave in; we fought back and staggered to our feet—a shaken but gallant giant.

Some things have been worse this time. The subway-L system broke down and still is a rolling ruin. Twelve years ago it kept going, somehow. This year's subzero temperatures and continuing high winds also have made things even harder for snow-fighting crews.

And the snow has kept on snowing. That's the worst insult of all. Is there no end to the stuff?

On the other hand, the toll of storm-connected deaths in the Chicago area was more than forty in the 1967 blizzard, contrasted with about twenty-five this time. And even the city's main arteries in 1967 congealed into wastelands—burial grounds of cars, trucks and buses, trapped in ice and snow and tossed around like toys.

"The drifts were worse then, and I can prove it," said a veteran of both storms who lives in suburban Clarendon Hills. "I shoveled seven feet from my garage door in 1967 and four feet this time."

That smasher of '67—and a follow-up surprise puncher of April, 1975—taught us a few unforgettable lessons. The City of Chicago apparently has mobilized more snow-removal equipment this time around—about 1,000 pieces compared with 600. We moved faster. We cleared big parking areas. But we still need more equipment. And we haven't yet learned to enforce parking rules, get cars off streets, and banish fallen snow before it turns into ice.

It took Chicago a long time to clear its roads and sidewalks and recover from the '67 disaster, and it will take a long time in '79, too. In both cases, the costs have been staggering and people have strained to the utmost.

The '67 invader came out of nowhere, almost, and in twenty-nine hours dumped a record twenty-three inches of snow. That was nearly three inches more than we absorbed over the weekend. But what difference do a few inches make in a snow mountain? Our 20.3 inches was heavy enough, and we started adding to it again Monday.

And when you throw in the nine inches that already was on the ground before the weekend whammy, we have a tremendous mess on our hands and under our feet. From that point of view, 1967 doesn't look all that overpowering.

The '67 crusher was so unexpected because, believe it or not, Chicago had been enjoying sixty-five-degree weather. That's right—June in January. Suddenly, the thing came out of the Pacific, slammed across the Rockies and sifted into open bedroom windows here.

Even then, the forecast was for about four inches of snow. "No one in his right mind would have predicted twenty-three inches," meteorologist Charles Feris said later. Right-minded people had expected that the storm would move faster than it did and pass swiftly over the city. Instead, it stalled right over our heads.

And it didn't go away until it wrecked the place. Expressways were knocked out and O'Hare Airport was socked in. Thousands of travelers were marooned, buses and cars coughed and died in fifteen-foot-high drifts, parked cars lay buried so deeply that they resembled snow sculpture, stranded workers huddled in downtown hotels. Schools and restaurants and shops closed, babies were delivered by telephone, hospital staffs struggled to keep going, helicopters dropped emergency medical supplies, 2,500 city workers toiled night and day to fight the snow. Exhaustion couldn't stop them.

The Loop was a cool heap of snow drifts, and some Chicagoans skiied to work. Others trudged through clogged streets, and took hours to get to work. But they got there. The cleansed air was incredibly fresh, the streets unbelievably quiet, the beauty of the snow mantle majestic.

Sound familiar? It should because it is more or less what happened again this year, beginning with a sneak punch. What started as a few inches of snow around midnight on Friday escalated with stunning strength when winds moved the storm center farther north than expected.

With time out for false comfort, the blizzard kept at it until 2:30 a.m. Sunday. Then the mercury dipped below zero and kept plummeting. To make things worse, winds began gusting up to thirty and forty miles an hour. In 1967, at least, it had been disarmingly warm before the blitz and reasonably restrained after that.

And this time, of course, the blizzard dumped on a city already groggy from a round of snowstorms. All in all, the problems have been "much worse" than in 1967, according to Mayor Bilandic.

One thing is sure: It was terrible then; it's horrible now. We didn't deserve it then; we don't deserve it now. But it happened then, and it has happened now. We survived that one, and we'll outlast this one.

And next time around? We'll beat that one, too. Probably it will be even worse, even bigger.

But it would be nice if we could arrange to put it off for 100 years or so. Make that 1,000 years.

—M.W. Newman

Sideviews

There were 6.5 million stories in the naked city and suburbs. Some heart-warming, some cold-hearted. Here's one of the former.

A Brink's truck was mired in the mess in front of a Jewel Food Store at 3435 S. Archer on Saturday, a sitting duck (or a golden goose) for the Snow Shoe Gang. But some Good Samaritans got there first.

The Brink's guards flagged down an Archer Av. bus and asked for help. Six passengers got off the bus to push and were joined by several Jewel employees. The bus went on, but the Brink's truck was freed after fifteen minutes.

(below) The collapsed roof of a warehouse at 1400 West Altgeld. (right) Snow is shoveled from the top of a building at 1415 West Fullerton as a precaution against the roof collapsing.

(above) Shoveling snow from the roof of Senn High School. (right) Clearing the roof of the Aetna Plywood Company. (far right) Digging out on the 3700 block of North Racine.

Sideviews

Kate Marshall, director of volunteers for the Little Brothers of the Poor, appealed for volunteers to take food to the elderly who couldn't get out. Almost twenty new persons volunteered, mothers with children, people stranded at home and suffering from cabin fever.

Gerry Gorman and Ellen Titra, graduate students from Loyola University, shop one day a week for the elderly. They added an extra day this week, digging out and driving in from Rogers Park to the order's headquarters at 1658 W. Belmont. But the monthly visits, just to chat, to 600 homes was canceled so volunteers could concentrate on getting hot meals to the elderly and taking others out by bus to supermarkets.

(left) Clearing the street from the alley westbound on Arthur between Fairfield and California. (right) Freeing autos from snowdrifts on 70th, just east of Pulaski. (below) Digging out at Wacker and Washington.

Sideviews

There were a blizzard of good deeds. Neighbors helped neighbors. Neighborhoods pitched in to dig out cars, clear streets, take food to shut-ins. Persons were helicoptered to hospitals, patients were carried in on stretchers to kidney dialysis machines, employees made herculean efforts to get to jobs and stayed on, working long hours to compensate for undermanned staffs.

Morris Howe, 69, of 2653 W. Carmen, has an artery problem, but he had been cooped up so many days and he needed to get to the grocery store. He persuaded his next-door neighbor, Isabelle Hanson, to accompany him to a nearby supermarket. She got her nephew, Jack Hetland, to come along.

After getting the food, the three were on the way home when Howe was stricken and fell to the snow. Charles R. Wiltgen, 40, of 4949 N. Bell, was passing by. A big man of 230 pounds, Wiltgen went to Howe's aid, picked him up, put him over his shoulder and carried him two blocks to Swedish Covenant Hospital.

(far left) Shoveling snow at 1534 North Elston. (left)
Digging out the family car on West Foster. (above)
Neighbors pitch in to clear their street.

(left) Teenagers from the Woodlawn Organization work with two city tractors to unclog side streets and dig out cars. (above) Residents of the 3600 block of North Racine turn out in mass as they work to clear their cars from the snow.

(above) Residents at Sedgwick and Webster dig out.
(right) Shoveling a path across the infield at Wrigley
Field.

*A snowblower is used to clear the sidewalk in
front of residences on North Racine near Waveland.*

Digging Out: Suburbs

Clearing snow from the roof of a home in Glen Ellyn.

Sideviews

"We started out with only about five inches on the ground when the snow began January 12," said Robert B. Pierce, village manager of Park Forest, a southern suburb. "We also had more parkways and places in the street to put the snow because we had less to contend with. The snowplows were able to keep all the main routes open all the time, and most of the minor streets were mostly passable. Only a few were impassable."

(left) One of the many garages in Oak Park that suffered damage because of heavy accumulation of snow on the roof. (below left) Schaumburg's Unimog plows snow and fights fires. (below) This Elk Grove Village homeowner has some digging out to do.

Sideviews

"We think we are keeping up," said Robert P. Palmer, the city manager of Elmhurst, a western suburb. "Nobody is seriously inconvenienced. Certainly the curbs are not showing on any street, but even the side streets are open to two passing cars. One problem is that there's no place to put the snow.

"It's very expensive to pick it up and haul it away."

(above left) Snowed in in Elk Grove. (left) Intersection of Elmhurst and Touhy Avenue in Elk Grove. (above) Shoveling off the roof of a garage at Pulaski near 69th. (top above) Storm was too much for this snowplow in Hoffman Estates on Hillcrest Road.

Snowplow coming over the hill
on Roselle Road in Hoffman Estates.

Operation Snowplow

(above) Looking down on parking lots at Sox Park. (left) Salt is loaded into trucks from a pile near Lake Shore Drive and the Chicago River as city crews try to get city streets back to normal.

Sideviews

Francis Degnan, commissioner of streets and sanitation for Chicago, says things are better than in 1967, as far as street clearing is concerned. You have to keep in mind that there are 4,000 miles of streets, the equivalent, he points out, of driving to Los Angeles and back. (If we could drive there, we sure as hell wouldn't come back.)

"In 1967 it took us two or three weeks to clear the streets. We're far ahead of 1967," he said.

There are 1,000 pieces of removal equipment on the streets, some from as far away as Buffalo, Cleveland, Montana and Quebec.

City crew clearing the intersection at 51st and King Drive.

(above) City crew clearing the streets around Wacker and Michigan. (right) The National Guard works at clearing the streets at Lake and LaSalle.

(left) Clearing Janssen Street between Grace and Byron. (below) Working to clear the main street of Archer at Laramie.

(above) Chicago's Snow Command in operation at Central and Montrose working its way toward Roosevelt Road. (left) City crews continue their massive clean-up effort along Fullerton Avenue just west of Sheffield.

Sideviews

Mayor Bilandic, occasionally in turtleneck and ski sweater, popped up on so many television news programs that he seemed to be auditioning for an anchorman's spot. But psychologists and psychiatrists said that the mayor, as a father figure, was doing the right thing: We citizens were comforted, consciously or subconsciously, to see him on the job and to hear his reassurances.

On one series of appearances, he announced a plan for moving cars from the clogged thoroughfares and side streets to cleared parking lots. The plan became known to some skeptics as Operation Snow Job. It turned out that only about half of the designated 103 school yards and lots had been cleared. The mayor expressed his regret, revised the list and said that heads would roll for the boner.

Payloader is used to clear snow and free vehicles in the 1600 block of North Wells.

Oh, To Be Rolling Again! How Some Got Wheels

They don't call Chicago the City of the Big Shoulders for nothing. There are bus drivers, limo drivers, cab drivers and everyday drivers to testify to that in the wake of Blizzard '79.

South Sider Amberlina Wicker called The Sun-Times to crow about the triumph of a small band of passengers stranded for two hours at a stop on 79th St. in front of a bus terminal.

The group of about twenty-five people had seen buses going west and into the terminal, but none leaving going east. Finally, seven people marched into the terminal and demanded a bus.

A dispatcher met the angry group, and after five minutes, sent a bus out to pick up the twenty-five shivering commuters.

• • •

Elsewhere, new transportation techniques were developed. The "divide and conquer" tactic was being employed at many bus stops where passengers split into one or more groups to pound at the front and back doors for admittance.

One driver reportedly counted passengers entering at the rear of his buses, making announcements periodically that he expected "$1.50 in fares to be passed forward at once." Passengers obliged.

Other cold commuters came to the stops with handmade signs to alert passing motorists headed their way. Motorists and cab drivers already hired often slowed to shout out their destinations, taking in as many passengers as possible.

• • •

One would-be bus rider on Sheridan Rd., who had spent an hour watching large cars pass with only a driver inside, said, "Now I understand hijackers. I feel like jumping into those cars and screaming, 'Take me to work!' "

In Evanston, thirty Northwestern University students led by Robin Sebur had volunteered to help the CTA shovel out tracks and switching points, hoping to get the Evanston Rapid Transit lines moving.

• • •

At least two people found some humor in Blizzard '79. There is a mysterious "ice artist" who has carved out smiling faces and "Help!" signs on the snow-covered cars in Lincoln Park.

And one local driver, Celeste Busk, says the blizzard is better than singles bars. "I've been having nothing but fun. I had eight young men pushing my car out of a drift this weekend. I loved it!"

—Cynthia Dagnal

Nasty weather brings out the nasties

For a city covered with frozen water, Chicago has a lot of folks near the boiling point.

The irritation level seems to be rising steadily with each new layer of snow.

People who made light of the Blizzard of '79 are laughing less. Others scream at each other, almost coming to blows, in the daily contests for space and position.

Frustrating personal experiences touch off outspoken criticism of City Hall's failure to bring Chicago back to normal.

In short, the weeklong struggle with mountains of snow is bringing out the nasties.

Some examples of the causes:

● ● ●

CONFUSION—On the Southwest Side, several businesses paid $4,000 to clear snow from their private parking lots, three blocks of S. Kilbourn and a few side streets. Their efforts were nullified by city trucks that dumped more snow back into the same spaces.

Tom Fitzgerald, director of manufacturing for Litho-Strip Co. at 4800 S. Kilbourn, said nearby streets were cleared Tuesday on the theory it would be "good public relations." But Fitzgerald said city trucks brought in more snow from elsewhere Tuesday night.

When complaints arrived, the city shifted the snow to nearby Archer Park on Wednesday and Thursday. Friday morning, the business lots and streets once again were full of snow brought in by city trucks.

"Last night was the second time," Fitzgerald said Friday. "We're getting nowhere with Streets and Sanitation."

● ● ●

SARCASM—Rapid-transit passengers waiting at stops along the Howard St. L were infuriated Friday morning by the conduct of a well-dressed woman riding one of the trains.

At each stop, as people tried to squeeze aboard her train, she would yell, "You dumb turkeys. There are ten or eleven trains coming right behind us. Get out of the door and let this train move."

Responded one woman passenger, "Everybody's suffering. I just wish you'd keep your big mouth shut."

● ● ●

THAT DESERTED FEELING—Dale Pontius, retired Roosevelt University political science professor, lives at 5704 S. Harper. Big traffic tie-ups on snow-clogged 57th St. Thursday and Friday prompted him to call the office of Alderman Ross Lathrop (5th). There he was told that all city snow-removal equipment had been pulled out of the 5th Ward.

Pontius, who said that 57th St. is in bad shape from Stony Island to Cottage Grove, commented, "A bonfire should be built under City Hall."

Sharon Foster, aide to Alderman Lathrop, said all snow-removal equipment was pulled out of the ward Thursday afternoon. City officials have promised that it will return Saturday and operate around the clock through Monday.

● ● ●

PULLING RANK—Commuters were lined up at the downtown station of the Chicago & North Western Railroad waiting for the train doors to open so they could board. A young man wearing an Army field jacket walked to the front of the line.

The waiting commuters cut loose with a few choice words, grabbed the man and hustled him to the rear. Only after things calmed down did the man get a chance to explain that he was the engineer, checking the train doors.

● ● ●

THE COLLAPSE OF COURTESY—Early in the snow emergency, motorists generally were willing to yield when their cars met on streets narrowed to one-lane traffic. But attitudes are changing.

On N. Sheffield, two male drivers refused to give way to each other. Both jumped out of their cars, shook their fists and started yelling. One shouted that he wasn't backing up because he had spent six hours digging his car out of the snow. "I'm not backing up," screamed the other. "It took me nine hours."

—Harlan Draeger

*An auto lies overturned in a snowbank at Argyle and
Ridgeway, possibly dumped there by irate neighbors.*

BuRck
1979 CHICAGO SUN TIMES

City of the big shoulders

A woman in a wheel chair is helped over a huge
snow pile in the 2700 block of north Clark Street.

Trudging to work through the drifts along the
594 extension of the JFK that leads toward O'Hare.

Sideviews

"It's been a gigantic pain in the neck, but a profitable one," said Robert J. Jacobs, executive director of the Illinois Gasoline Dealers Association. "Service stations have been terribly, terribly busy. In this very cold weather combined with the deep snow, everything that can go wrong with a piece of towing equipment or an automobile does."

There were above-and-beyond acts. At Harlem and Foster, one group of service station employees tried to clean up side streets on the way back from service calls. Ernie Tagliere led a group of twenty-six dealers who did free snowplowing on side streets.

Jacobs conceded there was some overcharging by opportunistic dealers. Many have run out of gas because resupply trucks couldn't get to them, "but dealers have come out ahead financially by working hard and risking their equipment."

"Business has been great," said Steve Michielutti, mechanic at Central Mobil Service Center, 5601 Diversey. "We have a two-day backup for tows. We get about twenty calls for tows a day. We've had to turn down a lot of jumps and tows because of the backup. We ask the callers if they can wait for a couple of days, and they say, 'Hell, no!' "

James Jana (pronounced Yah nah), director of the Chicago Dance Laboratory, offers some advice on proper ways to walk in the snow. He proposes what he calls the Penguin Theory of Walking.

"Don't take long, striding steps," Jana said. "Take short, quick steps.

"Maintain a low center of gravity. Try to feel your stomach between your waist and your knees. . ."

Between your waist and your knees?

"Yes. Dancers try to keep their center of gravity low."

Proceed.

"Maintain your arms out slightly to the side, like a little penguin's wings, so if you fall, your arms are engaged to break it."

Makes sense.

"Also, look down just with an eye movement. Many people, especially the elderly, look down directly in front, which bends their head down and brings their body weight forward so that it's easier to fall. And relax. Don't raise your shoulders when you walk. That makes your back colder, your breath more shallow and makes you tense and you feel the cold more."

Thank you.

(left) Spinning tires and clouds of exhaust fill the air as a small car tries to free itself from the ice and snow while passing a stalled car on North State Parkway at Goethe. (below left) Eastbound traffic on Armitage at Sheffield is backed up for blocks as a result of an L train derailment at Armitage stop.

(above) 46th Ward Workers clearing Janssen Street between Grace and Byron. (left) A man pushes his bicycle along Larabee south of Armitage Avenue.

(right) Snowmobiler cruises down Grand Avenue near State Street. (below) A cross-country skiier finds the going easy on Sedgewick Street near Wisconsin on the North side.

78

(above) Wacker and Dearborn. (left) Slushy
streets at Michigan and Wacker.

(left) Heading home from Randolph and Michigan in the frozen heart of Chicago. (below) Walking slow and steady past the huge mounds of snow on the east side of Michigan Avenue north of Washington. (right) Pedestrians make their way east across Michigan Avenue at South Water.

*Snow and winds hamper pedestrians
at Wacker and South Water Streets.*

Commuter Refrain: What Happened?

The Blizzard of '79 may have been the worst winter storm in Chicago's modern history. Even the best man-made equipment sometimes fails in such extreme weather. The heroes of the blizzard were the people who worked long, sleepless hours, many of them in subzero weather, trying to get the streets cleared and the buses and trains moving.

BUT: Could more have been done to prevent the transportation mess?

Or, do we expect too much from the transportation system?

The answer to one question always seems to lead to another.

First, it isn't just one operation, so you can't generalize about performance. Every one of the hundreds of municipalities in the six-county area has its own snow-removal operations. So do the townships, the counties and the state. Each of the dozens of bus systems, the commuter railroads and the CTA are responsible for their own operations. The Regional Transportation Authority is responsible for all performance of all those public transit carriers, but it doesn't run them itself.

It's safe to say that performance ran from good to stinko.

Take the railroads. The flurry of excuses for late and stalled trains came as thick as the flakes of the blizzard itself.

Through it all, one railroad—the Burlington Northern—kept reasonably close to its schedule.

On Tuesday morning, several lines were tossing their schedules out the window, running a train whenever they could, with delays of up to two hours. But eighty-five percent of the BN trains were on time. Only a few Burlington trains ran as late as ten or fifteen minutes behind schedule, according to BN officials.

The reason their trains continued to run is more than luck. In a word: planning. Burlington officials said that when the ferocity of the blizzard first became apparent last weekend, they put their plans into effect. Additional crews were called in from as far away as Kansas City. The maintenance crews were put on twelve-hour shifts and crews were working around the clock, digging out and thawing frozen switches.

Trains sitting in the yards were fired up and warmed for four-hour periods. When they got cold, they were turned on again. Locomotives with cabooses were turned loose to keep the mainlines clear of snow. Operating crews were surveyed by phone the day before the first onslaught of rush-hour commuters to find out where gaps would have to be filled.

"The planning is the biggest thing. You have to be ready for (the bad weather). You can't just wait until it happens," said E. R. Craven, the railroad's regional vice president.

Sounds expensive. How much does it all cost? Craven seemed surprised by the question. His response was that he didn't know, and that it didn't matter. It was a problem that would have to be worked out later.

Transportation experts say that you can't really compare the diesel-powered commuter railroads with the electric-powered trains such as the CTA's and the Illinois Central Gulf's.

The reason is that the trains are run by electric motors mounted beneath the cars and likely to be clogged and shorted out by snow and water, or corroded by salt. About half of the 900 cars in the CTA's rapid transit fleet were disabled on Wednesday by the problems.

But can't the electrical apparatus be enclosed in a protective casing? CTA officials say that the electrical motors need ventilation, and no matter how many baffles are built in, moisture will find its way in.

Do outside experts agree? Officials of transit car building companies for the most part declined to discuss the matter, even off the record. The one official who would comment, made apparently contradictory statements: The rapid-transit car was designed to operate in these conditions, he said. But he quickly pointed out that automobiles sometimes can't be started in such extreme weather.

That analogy often is used to justify transit equipment failures, but looking at it from another perspective: If you drove 200,000 people to the Loop every day in your car, it would be worthwhile to find a way to make sure your car starts.

The CTA also has problems with ice forming on its third rail, cutting off power to the transit cars. Attempts have been made to apply an antifreeze to the third rail or use heating elements, but the results have been inconclusive, the CTA says. Some rapid-transit systems in other cities have a covered third rail, open on one side for the train's power pickup shoes. But that has been ruled out here because of the costs of conversion.

Aside from the equipment problems, did the CTA prepare adequately like the Burlington Northern? CTA officials said it did, running trains constantly over its tracks to keep them clear of ice and snow, even during off-hours. The snow just piled up too fast, they said.

But one has to wonder. On Friday, the CTA admitted it didn't have snow plows that could handle the job. It had disposed of old locomotives and cars that were equipped with plows. But why it didn't obtain plows that could attack the big drifts? The portions of the rapid-transit system that suffered the worst problems—the Skokie Swift, Evanston line and Howard line between Howard St. and Wilson Ave., is where the tracks run at ground level or on an embankment. That's where the snow easily accumulates and good plows would have been most useful. On Monday, after the storm, the CTA quickly began building small plows made of plywood.

Boston took snow-fighting measures, including the purchase of two jet snow blowers, following its crippling blizzard last year. The CTA says that jet blowers tried in Chicago have been ineffective; Boston says it hasn't needed to use them yet this year.

It was the accumulation of snow, rather than equipment failures, that hit the CTA's bus system the hardest, according to the agency. Almost all of its 2,100 buses were operating, but schedules were chaotic because of streets choked with snow and abandoned cars.

The CTA once plowed streets used by its buses, but that job was taken over by the city several years ago on the grounds that it was more efficient and economical to consolidate the job. The CTA's bus drivers' union disagrees, arguing that the streets seemed to get cleared faster when the CTA had the responsibility.

James McDonough, now the CTA chairman, said that Mayor Daley ordered him to do an exhaustive study of snow-removal operations following the severe 1967 winter storm. McDonough, then Streets and Sanitation commissioner, said that after visiting many cities, he concluded that no one does it better then Chicago. Still, a number of recommendations emerged from the study, including the assignment of high priorities to streets that carry CTA buses. Questions now are being asked about how well those recommendations have been executed. Major bus routes, such as Sheridan Rd., still were a mess days after the blizzard ended.

The city still apparently was trying to learn from experience when it handed a $90,000 contract to politically connected Ken Sain to recommend improvements following last year's snow storms. City Hall says that Sain's recommendations for improved snow removal equipment and procedures were adopted. Others say that the results speak for themselves.

Then there is the question of whether the city's side streets should be plowed. Residents in Northbrook and many other suburbs awoke Monday morning after more than twenty inches of snow had fallen to find their residential streets cleared. Northbrook village manager Robert Weidaw said it is not fair to compare the city with most suburbs, which have ample off-street parking, permitting easy plowing of side streets. Weidaw and McDonough separately said that plows are too wide to negotiate the narrow city streets that typically have cars parked on both sides. The problem becomes one of car relocation rather than snow removal.

Even so, Bilandic promised that a side street clearing program would be quickly undertaken.

The obvious question that no one seems to ask is why isn't a plow designed and purchased that can handle the side streets?

All these problems were caused by factors that no one could control—snow followed by bitter cold temperatures. But city and transportation officials have brought perhaps the biggest problem on themselves: credibility. Once lost, it may be harder to regain than clear streets and smooth-running trains.

Thousands of commuters were disappointed, angry and disgusted when they tried to catch trains and buses after they heard inadequate or incorrect information on radio or TV, supplied by officials. Many city residents worked hard to dig out and drive their cars to school yard lots which the city incorrectly said had been plowed.

Bilandic has apologized for that mistake, and the Regional Transportation Authority has pledged to improve communications with its passengers.

RTA board member Dan Baldino went so far as to suggest the RTA use its own money instead of federal grants to avoid red tape and get the project under way. "The public no longer will tolerate this," he said.

—Dennis Byrne

The evening "slush" hour looking north from State and Lake.

84

"Pass the word"

A dangerous practice as commuters ride on a coupling between two elevated train cars on the Ravenswood line near the Fullerton station.

The motorman of a disabled Lake-Dan Ryan CTA train views the predicament near Ridgeland in Oak Park.

(left) Burlington Northern works at clearing their yards of snow. (below) CTA riders helped drivers watch for troubles—these, on Sheridan Road, stood with their noses almost pressed against the windshield.

(below) Rush hour train riders are packed close together on the trains leaving the State and Lake L platform. (left) Waiting for a bus at Archer and Western. (right) Crowds of commuters jam the North Western station during evening rush hour. (below right) Waiting for IC trains.

(far left) Waiting for a bus on State Street. (left) Waiting for the bus at Fullerton west of Damen. (below) Commuters waited for as much as four hours for trains at the Fullerton L platform.

(above) Waiting for the bus at Lake and Wabash.
(left) Stranded by an L derailment, commuters at
State south of Wacker turn to the buses.

Business—As Usual?

Hospitals, which deal with crisis, carried on. Some had staff shortages of forty to fifty percent immediately after the storm, some elective surgery was postponed, and some patients, fearful of going out into the cold, were permitted to stay in the hospital for a longer than normal time.

The Housewares show is not unfamiliar with Chicago catastrophes. It was in 1967 when this biggest of all shows was all set for its really biggest show in the new McCormick Place. Unfortunately, McCormick Place burned down, leaving the show in ashes.

In 1979, it was a blizzard. Maybe next time, a plague of locusts.

This is the largest merchandising extravaganza there is. It is closed to the public, but 60,000 buyers and industry representatives gather together to buy and sell for thousands of retail stores. This year there were 1,830 exhibitors (up from 1,588 last year) and the show was to last from Sunday the 14th through Thursday.

Dolph Zapfel, the managing director, said the exhibitors had their wares in place when the storm hit. Some of the 19,000 buyers were delayed or deterred, Zapfel's not sure how many. Sunday and Monday were slow, Tuesday picked up and Wednesday and Thursday were big business days. The Housewares show was not a disaster.

And all this talk about its picking up and heading toward the Sun Belt is poppycock. The Housewares people just signed a contract through 1983 at McCormick Place, which has more space than any other hall in the country. Coupled with Chicago's bountiful hotel rooms, commerce can put up with natural disasters.

O.J. Simpson can run through all the airports for as long as he likes, but a treadmill would have been more productive for periods last week. The Hertz rental-car people would only say that business was down and cars were missing.

A spokesman for Budget was more forthcoming. He said its business was down fifty percent the first few days after the storm, that cars were stranded throughout the area, that the combination of snow and cold hampered starting or made it impossible, and that the dig-out of lots was continuing.

Hotels: There was room in the inns.

Most were booked solid for the Housewares show, 22,000 downtown and 8,000 near O'Hare Airport, but there were many no-shows.

A.M. Quarles, executive vice president of the Hotel and Motel Association of Chicago, said it was too early to total up the effect of the storm.

John Brisca, a public relations representative for the Hilton hotel chain, gave some examples. The Conrad Hilton and the Palmer House, he said, were sold out, but on Monday night 1,200 of 2,300 rooms in the Hilton were empty; at the Palmer House, 500 of 2,053 rooms were vacant. All because of no-shows. Only seventeen of ninety-two maids were able to make it to work on that Monday. The Hilton and Palmer House rallied quickly. The Hilton was down by only 400 rooms by Tuesday, and the Palmer House was full. Both hotels provided rooms for about 200 employees who couldn't get home.

The Ambassador East estimates a loss of about $8,000 because of the storm. The guests were understanding and the staff marvelous, an executive reported.

Quarles said cancellation of banquets and meetings was a major setback for hotels.

At the O'Hare Hilton, general manager Lynn Montjoy, who is accustomed to dealing with weather-induced foul-ups, said the hotel usually has thirty to forty meetings a day. They were scratched left and right.

But the stranded travelers were co-operative and tolerant. "The first day people are uptight," Montjoy said. "The second day they relax a bit, and the third day they consider themselves members of your staff."

Montjoy said everyone, including a devoted staff, behaved in exemplary fashion. He singled out housekeeper Eva Lee Hoskins, who was written up in the Wall Street Journal, for special recognition. Normally a maid cleans sixteen rooms. Mrs. Hoskins took care of a marathon seventy-nine on Sunday.

"Of course," she acknowledged, "I didn't dust too well in all the corners."

It paid off. Her day's wages rose from $25.50 to $138.48.

Robert P. Leroy, vice president and general manager of the Drake Hotel, said his hostelry fared well, from eighty to ninety percent occupancy. "The spirit of co-operation within the staff was great. This type of thing can improve morale. We were not hurt badly at all," he said.

"Contrasted to 1967, when we didn't get deliveries, we handled this blizzard much better," said James F. Sheerin, Hilton senior vice president. "It was much better than in the past. The only thing we ran short of was honey-dip chicken at the O'Hare hotel.

"I just talked to our man in Hawaii, on the big island. They just had sixty-one inches of rain. That could be 610 inches of snow, right up to the sixth floor. They have problems in Hawaii, too," Sheerin said, trying to be of some comfort.

But in Hawaii, even sixty-one inches of rain sounds good.

Chicago public and parochial schools were closed all week, as were most schools in the suburbs.

The Yellow Cab Co. was offering a $25 bounty for any person who would dig out their abandoned taxis and drive them in. (Most had the keys in them.) The Checker Taxi Co. said by midweek it had recovered about 150 of 200 cabs stuck in the snow and abandoned. Without the snow, the company would have 1,400 to 1,500 cabs careening around the city streets. On Monday, a spokesman said 1,100 cabs were slogging about. There were reports of gouging by drivers, who were charging, some explained, for the extra time taken and the extraordinary conditions. Riders were complaining and paying.

The costs of the Blizzard of '79 are astronomical.

Although there was no official tally or estimate, sources at City Hall were saying that the City of Chicago had already spent the $2.76 million budgeted for snow removal and is certain to surpass last year's $7.2 million expenditure. The

Firefighters encrusted with ice battle a blaze.

ers, our business has been affected and it will make it difficult to reach expectations in our January sales."

Larry Buckmaster, president of the Chicago and Illinois Restaurant Association, said it this way:

"The weather has been an absolute, complete tragedy."

Elaborating on his "absolute, complete tragedy" statement, Larry Buckmaster of the restaurant association said the restaurant industry had been hit hardest of any part of the economy. You can't make up for lost meals.

"The Indian Trail Restaurant in Winnetka, which normally

federal money will help, but the total bill may pass $10 million.

In the devastated private sector, some marginal businesses are sure to go under.

John Coulter, research director of the Chicago Association of Commerce and Industry, estimated that $1.1 billion in sales and more than $200 million in wages had been lost the week after the storm.

The absentee rate was high, forty to fifty percent at some businesses, and shoppers were scarce in many places. On Monday the Loop, even State Street, that great and vital merchandising street, looked about as busy as a remote trading post in the Klondike.

There were different ways of saying business was lousy.

A spokesman for Marshall Field & Co. said it this way:

"Due to the snow and resulting difficulties in transportation that has hindered our employees, and also our custom-

serves 1,000 persons, had three diners on Saturday night," Buckmaster said. "It had to close for the first time in fifty years. The Tower Garden restaurant in Skokie had twelve customers. You never recover from these things. It was desperate and still is in the suburbs where parking can be impossible."

Many city restaurants are badly wounded by the storm, Buckmaster said. "The losses are in the millions of dollars, but we can't come up with a figure yet. Some are certain to go out of business, they have been hurt so bad."

The Coast Guard came to Carolyn Kozel's rescue Wednesday. So did a doctor and a nurse she didn't know.

The Crown Point, Indiana, woman is resting comfortably in Northwestern Memorial Hospital, although she and her newborn son are in a medically difficult situation.

Continued on page 98

(above) Reaching into a snow bank to retrieve some covered garbage. (left) Firemen push their truck, stuck in the snow. (right) Directing traffic at the intersection of State and Wacker.

The child was due March 3, but at 4:30 a.m. Wednesday, Mrs. Kozel suffered serious complications.

"I wanted her in a regional obstetrical center that deals with complicated pregnancies," Dr. John King, her obstetrician, said. "I wanted her and the baby in intensive care after the birth."

He called Prentice Women's Hospital and Maternity Center, one of three Chicago hospitals with intensive-care units for sick mothers and children and a transport service to the hospital that provides a doctor and nurse.

The snow made an ambulance ride impossible, so hospital personnel called the Coast Guard, which arranged a helicopter flight for Mrs. Kozel.

Cicero firefighter John Richter, 35, broke the law and became a hero.

Snowmobiles are prohibited on streets in the western suburb, but Richter took a ride around town on one last Sunday anyway.

"I saw a car on fire three blocks off the main thoroughfare," he said. "I saw a fire truck go toward it, and I followed. The truck got stuck. I told the lieutenant to give me one firefighter and some equipment and I'd put out the fire."

With that, Richter started something that kept him at the fire station from 6 p.m. Sunday until early Wednesday. He and another fireman on a second snowmobile became medical and fire rescuers. Ambulances would go to a main street and wait on a corner while Richter took an emergency medical technician by snowmobile to the patient.

"We carried two blankets, two sheets, two towels and a stokes basket to secure the patient to a toboggan we carried behind the snowmobile," Richter said. "We'd pull them through to the ambulance. I remember I carried one woman with a broken shoulder, a man with a stroke and a third, very ill person."

He helped dig out fire hydrants, carried fire officials to fires to estimate how much equipment was needed and he ran errands.

—Paul Galloway

Pedestrians on State Street dream of the days when they can check out bikinis on the beach.

'It's Time for Spring'

Dear Margaret:

You asked me to write you a letter and tell you what it's like to live with bad snow, so here goes. First of all, I hope the weather is good in Sacramento, California, because it sure stinks here.

Up to nineteen inches of snow is predicted today. Everyone is socked in, except those who were smart enough to leave town for a warm place before O'Hare Airport was shut down. Air Jamaica's North American manager, Trudy Newnam, said business is very good. American Airlines reservations clerks advise making reservations *now* for March flights to Acapulco.

It's a nice day in Miami Beach. The temperature is in the mid-seventies and kids are running around in shorts and no shoes. Out of curiosity I called Helen Mericle, a long-time North Miami Beach resident. She reports that it's hot enough to run the air conditioners at night and that the neighbors' trees are covered with big pink flowers.

Here the trees and the streets are socked in. About twenty-five people on the 5200 block of S. Justine are outside shoveling each other's cars out from the curbs. It was spontaneous, according to Matthew Wachna, who lives on the corner. First one came out to shovel, then another, and it soon became a block project.

Kevin Horan, a Sun-Times photographer, parked his car on Stockton Dr. in Lincoln Park and walked over to Lake Shore Dr. to take a picture of the traffic. When he came back, he found his car had been buried by a snowplow.

Avis and Hertz have rented all the cars with snow tires.

Bathing suits are selling very well at Saks Fifth Avenue. Sears, Roebuck's Loop store is having a run on long underwear. One sales clerk said that she couldn't get longjohns on the counter fast enough, and that although the store stocked three times as many woolies as last year, it's starting to run low.

Alper-Richman Furs Ltd., 645 N. Michigan, is doing great business. "I sold four men's fur coats last Saturday," said Burton Richman. "One fellow bought a mink coat and a coyote jacket. That's about $7,000 to $8,000."

Snowblowers are big out in the suburbs. The Ace Hardware store at 1020 Grove Mall, Elk Grove Village, got fifteen snowblowers Friday and sold fifteen snowblowers by Friday night. "I could have sold 215," said store manager Bob Miller.

Lynne Frost, of Elk Grove Village, dug herself out of the driveway and drove there to buy a blower. "It took two hours to get there. I got stuck a few times. And then the snowblower wouldn't fit in the car," she said.

I looked out the window and saw another kind of help. A guy in a red VW hatchback pulled up to the salt box on Wacker and Wabash, loaded four bucketfuls into his car, and then took off.

Another reporter here saw a mailman at Kimbark and 56th St. delivering his mail by sled.

Jim Vrettos, owner of Evergreen Fine Foods, 3203 N. Broadway, said his trucks couldn't deliver groceries, though he was trying to hire kids to walk them home. "I called the ward superintendent's office and he said that if I tried to send a truck down a side street, I'd get what I deserved," Vrettos said. He also said that people were stocking up in anticipation of being socked in.

I asked CTA spokesman Tom Buck, who is snowed in at his home in Evanston, what the view was like. "My barbecue kettle looks like R2D2," he replied.

I know you like me to tell you all the cute things your grandchildren say. I can't do that, but I'll close with the assessment of another kid. Deirdre Rhyce, who is 3½, was finishing dinner last night when she told her mother: "I think it's time for spring to come tomorrow."

Amen, and please hurry.

I'll write again soon. I think I'll have lots of time because we'll be snowed in.

—Laura Green

Sideviews

Some comparisons with the 1967 storm from Steve Kahn, a forecaster with the National Weather Service: "We did not match the 8.2 inches that fell in the six hours (from 6 a.m. to noon) in '67. The storm in 1967 was more intense during the day, and it struck on a Thursday, a working day. People started getting trapped, rushed for home and blocked the streets with their stalled cars. The winds were stronger in 1967, and it was a wetter snow. It was harder to push around and easier to get stuck. The day-before temperature in 1967 was in the sixties. Just before the 1979 storm, it was below zero."

And after, of course, we tied the Twentieth-Century record for cold, when the temperature reached nineteen below zero at 4:25 a.m. Monday.

If the roads weren't blocked and O'Hare hadn't been at a near standstill, the entire population might have split for Phoenix or Fort Lauderdale, permanently.

Sideviews

One positive result of the Great Blizzard of '79 may be that we won't have to hear any more of those boring stories about the Great Blizzard of '67.

A negative result will be hearing about this stinking storm for years to come.

(left) Skating at the Waveland ice rink.
(above) This young man suffers from "cabin fever" in Elk Grove.

Sideviews

Well, it was quite an experience, and I want to invite everyone down to Houston to visit me next winter.

As We Saw It:

Snowbound auto
ticketed on
Lincoln,
south of
Dickens.

Mike Royko
Mayor's big snow job

It has become clear that Mayor Bilandic is running for re-election on an image of being The Great Human Snow Shovel.

During the entire blizzard weekend, I don't think even one TV news show went by that didn't feature Bilandic, staring into the camera like a taxidermist's fish while describing City Hall's heroics in preventing the wolves and bears from roaming down from the North Woods and devouring us.

"Dis is a worse storm den we had in 1967," he kept explaining, as if the recent heavy snowfall were a personal achievement. "But we're gunna get all duh snow otta dare, and duh city is gunna work and keep workin'."

Most of the TV interviewers were so thrilled to have Bilandic doing a stand-up imitation of the late Mayor Richard J. Daley that they didn't have the sense to ask the obvious question, one of which might have been:

• Say, Mr. Mayor, what would have happened if all this snow had arrived on a Tuesday or Wednesday, instead of on a weekend?

The answer, if honestly given, would have been that this city would have been in total chaos, as it was in 1967 when thousands of cars were left abandoned in the middle of streets, and people walked like refugees to their homes.

If this storm had occurred on a workday, the city would have been completely shut down for days afterwards. Even the snow-removal crews wouldn't have been able to get to their equipment. With the subzero cold that followed the snow, the big problem for many people would have been survival, not movement.

Fortunately for Bilandic and the rest of us, the blizzard began at the start of a weekend, giving most people a chance to get home before the worst of it hit.

Because of that lucky timing, the city snow crews dealt with roads that were almost traffic free. The problem of stranded motorists was greatly reduced.

But even with an entire weekend to clean things up, the city was barely moving by Monday. The Chicago Transit Authority provided far more excuses than it did service. The major expressways, while open, were still covered with dangerous patches of ice.

And the only reason some people were able to get to their jobs on Monday was that most of them stayed home and didn't even try. Had everyone tried to go to work or school, most of them wouldn't have made it.

• Another line of questioning could have gone this way: Mr. Mayor, after floundering through several brutal winters, why do we keep pretending that we can handle heavy snowstorms? Why hasn't City Hall acquired modern snow-removal equipment? Why haven't we looked at Minneapolis, Montreal and other cold cities to see how they routinely handle even worse storms?

But if he answered those questions honestly, he might have to consider returning to the practice of law.

The answer is that it costs money for the equipment and manpower needed to dig out of the kind of winters we have been getting in recent years. And getting the money would mean raising our taxes.

In some cities, that would be an obvious, unavoidable solution. But City Hall has an embarrassing problem that it has created for itself.

The problem is that City Hall already has the manpower—at least in sheer numbers.

But it is a highly specialized work force. Its specialty is cranking out votes and winning elections for people like Bilandic and the aldermen.

As their reward, the political payrollers have lucrative jobs as building inspectors, sidewalk inspectors, electrical inspectors, milk inspectors, butcher scale inspectors and pothole inspectors. The Mirage Tavern series illustrated how many of them spend their time.

Many others act as a supplement to the law of gravity, using their elbows or feet to prevent desks in City Hall from drifting off into space.

Still others open doors and hold coats for aldermen and ward bosses, or strut about courtrooms ordering citizens to stand up when duh judge comes in.

They are very good at what they do, although you have to be quick if you are going to catch them in the act of doing it. But they're of little use when it comes to shoveling snow off the streets. Some haven't been on a city street since the last St. Patrick's Day parade.

So that is Bilandic's problem. If he says that he will have to raise our taxes to hire people to clear the streets of snow, some wise guy is bound to point at the plump city budget and ask why he has to hire more people when he already has so many on the payroll.

He would have a hard time mumbling his way out of that one. He couldn't very well admit that he can't ask good precinct captains to mess around with snow and ice. The salt might corrode their pinky rings.

Nor could he ask us to provide him two complete armies of payrollers—one to plow snow and the other to plow votes.

So he'll have to hope that we don't get another great snowfall; but that if we do, people will again fall for another great TV snow job from the Great Human Snow Shovel.

Mayor Michael Bilandic traveled in a police
four-wheel-drive vehicle during the snow days.

A safe and Sain winter

I would have thought that City Hall and Kenny Sain would be *proud* to show off the snow-removal study that Sain was paid $90,000 to write.

That is a lot of money. Many of the greatest books in history did not earn their authors $90, much less $90,000. Beethoven probably didn't make $100 for any of his symphonies. Even today, many fine writers slave for years over a piece of literature, only to accept a mere fraction of $90,000 to see it published.

If I ever write anything that is worth $90,000, I won't keep it secret, as City Hall has done with Sain's masterpiece. I'll throw a party and hand out autographed copies.

But City Hall has refused to let anybody look at Sain's snow-removal study.

That's a strange attitude, since we've paid for it. If a bookstore did that—took your money, then wouldn't give you a book—you would probably call the cops.

But City Hall apparently thinks it is OK for them to take our $90,000 and pass it on to Sain, then tell us that we can't see what we paid him to write.

It makes me wonder what they have to hide. Did Sain's snow-removal study recommend the making of giant snowmen or the holding of mass snowball fights?

Or did he write something like this? "Snow is pretty white stuff that is fun to ride a sled on. But if there is too much, it makes us slip and slide and fall down and go boom."

There has to be some reason for the secrecy. So I called City Hall and asked the city purchasing office if I could see the snow-removal study and any other studies that Sain has been paid for.

"Have you submitted your request in writing?" the lady said. "We have to have the particulars of your request in writing."

So I said: "If I put it in writing, will you pay me something for it?"

"What?" she said. "Pay you?"

"Well, sure. If you pay Kenny Sain $90,000 to write a snow-removal study, maybe you could see your way clear to slip me a few dollars for a written request. I'll make it a good written request. Would $15 be too much to ask?"

"I don't understand what you are talking about," she said, sounding agitated.

"OK, then just do me one favor. Tell me if there is any dirty stuff in Sain's study. You know, sex or something like that."

"Dirty stuff?"

"Sure. Lots of modern writing is pretty kinky. I thought maybe that was why it was being kept under the counter."

"Really, I have no idea what you are talking about."

"I just want to see the $90,000 study."

"Then you'll have to put your request in writing."

So I phoned Kenny Sain's office to ask him for a copy of his study, but he wasn't there and didn't return any of the phone calls.

I can't blame him. He's been mad at me for a long time because I once mentioned his late father while writing about him.

But it is impossible not to mention his father, or his uncle, if you are going to explain who Kenny Sain is to people who don't know him.

Sain is a good example of inherited clout, as it is practiced in Chicago politics.

His Uncle Harry was a machine alderman who ran the 27th Ward on the Near West Side. Harry's precinct captains could wring more votes out of a Skid Row flop-house than some reformers can produce in an entire ward.

Harry also managed to become a wealthy man on his modest alderman's salary. He had an insurance agency, and businessmen in his ward were his most devoted customers. They had to be devoted if they didn't want city inspectors overrunning them.

Then there was Kenny Sain's father, Frank. The machine made Frank sheriff of Cook County in the 1950s. Sheriff Sain was best known for snoozing in his office and hoping nobody would ask him any questions, because he never knew any answers.

When Kenny became old enough to go on a city payroll, his uncle arranged for him to go to work as an aide to Mayor Daley. But when Mayor Bilandic ascended to the throne, Kenny Sain went out into the world on his own, to practice law and scrounge a living.

However, City Hall likes to take care of people who go into the real world. It doesn't want them to wind up as panhandlers and embarrass the organization.

So it quietly slipped Kenny a $90,000 fee to do the mysterious snow-removal study that it won't let anybody read. That's almost three times as much as he was making when he was a full-time employee of the mayor's office.

He is also believed to have been paid for a couple of other studies, but nobody knows how much he received or what the studies were about, since they are also a secret. For all we know, Kenny Sain might be one of the highest paid unknown authors of our time.

Well, I hope that Bilandic will make Kenny's study public some day so we can all see what we got for our $90,000.

If nothing else, we can all use a good laugh. And if City Hall's recent efforts at snow removal were based on Kenny's study, then it is probably a comedy classic.

Please, Mr. Mayor, show us the Sain Study. Maybe Saturday Night Live will perform it.

Mayor Michael Bilandic after touring the city in a helicopter.

Brushoff for snow foe

Gary Coleman, an Air Force sergeant, has been taught a good lesson by Chicago.

When our blizzard hit, the word went out on national TV and radio that Chicago needed all the equipment it could hire.

Coleman lives in Dover, Delaware, which is a long way from Chicago. But he's young (23) and likes excitement and a challenge. So he called City Hall and asked if they could use him, a buddy and his truck, which is equipped with a seven-foot plow and a winch for towing cars.

"I was on leave anyway," he said, "and I wanted something to do. So I decided, what the heck, it might be fun to do. When I called, I told them the kind of equipment I had and that I'd come out there if they would guarantee my expenses.

"I wasn't interested in making a profit, just as long as I made enough for my gas, food and a motel room.

"The guy says to me 'Sure, come on out. There's plenty to do.' "

As everyone in Chicago knows, there was more than plenty to do for a snowplow, and there remains plenty to do today.

Coleman and his pal set out for Chicago taking turns behind the wheel, hoping to drive nonstop. It was slow-going when they hit the storm in Ohio. Along the way, they pulled some cars out of a ditch.

And along the way, Coleman found out that not everyone is as helpful as he tries to be.

"We stopped at a restaurant in Indiana and they were gouging on their prices because of the storm," he said. "Coffee was eighty cents. A regular breakfast came to $7.80.

"So our money was going faster than we had figured. But we knew we'd find work in Chicago."

After twenty-five hours of the kind of slippery driving that can give a person a fast ulcer, they skidded into Chicago. Coleman found a phone and called the purchasing department in City Hall, which has been hiring out-of-town equipment and men.

"They said they didn't know anything about me. They kept switching me from one person to another. It was the worst runaround I ever got.

"Somebody would tell me they needed help and they'd give me a phone number to call. So I'd call it, and he'd say, sure, they needed help, and he'd give me another phone number to call.

"Then I'd call that number, and he'd switch me to someone else. Then he'd give me another phone number to call.

"The way I was spending money on those phone calls, it was costing me more than that $7.80 breakfast.

"I finally got a guy on the phone and I told him that I was nearly broke, and that I'd be willing to work for the cost of my gas and motel and food.

"And he told me they didn't need me.

"I said, 'If you didn't need me, why didn't you tell me that when I was back in Delaware?'

"He said they already had all the equipment they needed.

"So there we were, stuck in Chicago and down to our last few dollars.

"Nobody would cash an out-of-town check, so I knew we'd have to earn some money if we were going to get back home.

"We plowed out a church lot and a food store lot in Chicago. Boy, everybody was piled up with snow. I don't see how they could say they didn't need any more help.

"Then we headed back toward home. In Indiana, we plowed a gas station and a truck stop motel. We earned enough money to get back here, even though I had exactly nineteen cents in my pocket when we finally made it.

"I've been watching my TV, and it still looks like you're snowed in. So I don't understand how they could say they didn't need us last week. It would have been different if I had been asking for a lot of money. But I was willing to just break even."

That was your mistake, young man. City Hall doesn't understand people who are willing to do anything free or at a bargain price.

When we asked City Hall why they gave you a brushoff, an aide to purchasing agent James Arnold snorted and said:

"Hah! I'll bet he came out here thinking he could make a thousand bucks, right?"

No, he said he was willing to work for enough to cover expenses?

"WHAT? He came here all the way from Delaware just to make expenses? What is he, nuts? I don't believe it."

See? That's what I mean about the Chicago attitude. And that is the lesson that young Sgt. Coleman has learned.

The next time you come out here, don't tell them you'll work for expenses.

Instead, tell them that you have just written a new twenty-three-page study on how Chicago should go about removing its snow. List a lot of well-known intersections (State and Madison, Lincoln and Belmont, etc.) and knowledgeably say they are high-priority intersections. Throw in a table of command and use a lot of bureaucratic jargon. Then print it in large type to make it look longer than it really is.

And tell City Hall that you want $90,000 for it.

That's the deal sly Kenny Sain has pulled off, to his profit and happiness, and nobody has said Kenny is nuts.

Because he got away with it, sly Kenny sure isn't nuts.

But those of us who paid for it are.

1st Ward snow-removal teams change shifts
at Wacker and Michigan.

The snow connection

In no other city would a record snowfall eventually be revealed to have a crime syndicate connection. But that's the kind of thing that makes Chicago unique.

The connection was alleged by the Wall Street Journal, which says that City Hall's Pete Schivarelli, the No. 1 man in our Snow Command, is a genuine underworld figure.

Schivarelli, the Journal says, is chummy with some of the city's leading young mafia goons, such as Anthony Spilotro, a very big gangster, although he is quite short; Harry Aleman, the city's most industrious professional hit man; Butch Petrocelli, who is Aleman's favorite hit-aide; and Turk Torello, an all-around meanie. None of them is the kind of person you'd want to meet unexpectedly on a moonlit night in a hedge next to your driveway.

The story said that Spilotro, Schivarelli and others might be plotting to muscle into the rock-music business and take over a famous and profitable rock band.

(I'm not sure what the objection to that would be. Considering the strange way many rock performers act in public, it might do them good to have the kind of discipline people like Spilotro can provide. Those punk rock musicians, who think it amusing to put pins in their own ears and noses, would not think it amusing if someone like Spilotro stuck the pins in for them.)

Schivarelli, 33, also finds time in his busy official schedule to manage a suburban nightclub, the Journal reported. If that is true, it just shows that city payrollers aren't the lazy louts that some people portray them to be. Anybody who can manage a nightclub, plot ways to muscle into the rock business, and still have time to supervise our snow removal, has to have his adrenalin going pretty good.

Schivarelli denies that he manages the nightclub, which can be expected, since a city official isn't supposed to hold that kind of moonlighting job.

He says that all he ever did for a nightclub owner was solve a personnel problem. There was a lot pilferage at the club, so he found a way to make the employees stop stealing. He didn't say how he accomplished that. Maybe he just stared at them and growled.

Based on his police record, that might be all Schivarelli would have to do. An ex-football player, he's been arrested a couple of times for allegedly trying to rearrange somebody else's limbs.

An investigator who tried to put Schivarelli behind bars told me about one of the arrests.

"Yeah, I got Schivarelli indicted a few years ago, along with a couple of his low-life pals, Rocco Lombardo and Mike Spilotro," the investigator said.

"Rocco is a nephew of Joey (the Clown) Lombardo, and Mike is Spilotro's younger brother.

"They were in a bar and some Greek guy spilled a drink and they didn't like it. Some words were exchanged, so they hit the Greek on the head with a bar stool.

"That should have settled the dispute, but then they did a real number on this guy. Schivarelli more or less danced a fandango on his chest, and the Greek was in terrible shape.

"So we got the indictments and got lucky when a straight judge set $100,000 bond.

"But then they go in and ask another judge to lower their bond, and he didn't think they looked like bad fellows, so he made the bond something like $500.

"Then we had the trial, and we even had witnesses who saw what they did to the guy, and remembered what they saw. But this judge didn't think they looked like bad fellows, either, so they were all found not guilty.

"Yeah, Schivarelli is well known to us. He hangs out all the time with the mob guys. And he comes from a heavy family himself. I think that when Sam DeStefano was hit, Schivarelli's uncle was suspected of being the hit man."

Considering his background and colorful acquaintances, it is impressive that Schivarelli has risen so quickly in city government to his present position as deputy commissioner of the Bureau of Sanitation. Maybe it was hoped that he would just scare the snow into going away.

Until I read the story in the Wall Street Journal, I wasn't aware that Schivarelli was thought to be a member of the syndicate's young social set. I had assumed that he was just another upwardly mobile cigar chomper, waiting for the day he, too, could do his own $90,000 snow-removal study.

In my ignorance, I had written things that were critical of his leadership and snow-removal talents.

Not anymore. Any city official who would dance a fandango on somebody's chest because of a mere spilled drink is not the kind of person I want to irritate.

So if you ask me, Schivarelli is doing a great job at Snow Command.

Sure, call me a coward. But remember, that man has 400 snowplows at his disposal. Why, it could be the middle of April before they found me under a snowbank.

Kup's Column

Remember the 1965 New York blackout, caused by a massive power failure, which forced people to stay home and led to an unusual baby boom nine months later? Will Chicago, as a result of Super Snow, have the same experience? (Or has shoveling been too taxing?) . . . The ERA has come full circle during the snow. Gil Stern found himself cursing old WOMAN winter!

Channel 2's Walter Jacobson delivered a stinging rebuke to Governor Thompson for leaving the state during the snow crisis for a vacation in Florida. His commentary was followed by an Eastern Airlines commercial, urging you to come to Florida! . . . Add snow glow: Bob Veles, owner of Lee-N-Eddie's Caterers, delivering huge boxes of fried chicken to police and fire headquarters and City Hall to employees working round the clock during the storm. And more than 5,000 Boy Scouts have volunteered to shovel the snow in front of fire hydrants and senior citizens' homes.

The mail indicates the public hasn't lost its sense of humor despite Super Snow. One postcard informs us that "a side street has been plowed open in your name." Another extends an invitation to a "bring your own shovel" party. Bob Orban pens, "We're all delighted to have a Polish Pope, but who ordered a Polish winter?" And Ivan Bunny assures us that Chicago always will have a lot of Snow—there are seventy-nine listed in the phone book.

This exasperating period of Super Snow and its sequel may be the proper time to break the news to you. According to one authority, "most people secretly love a blizzard because it gives them something to think about other than their normal problems, something basic, like survival." That's the word from Chicago's Dr. Jay H. Schmidt, who is writing a book, "Goodbye, Loneliness," in collaboration with author Paul Neimark. Feel better now? . . . And Gil Stern wonders aloud about Super Snow: "How can something so soft be so hard on us?"

Bob Conrad, after spending three months here to film six hours of his TV series, Duke, has returned to Hollywood. His last shot before the cameras was a personal message to NBC president Fred Silverman. Conrad held up a Sun-Times headline about the storm, "Worst ever," and added, "The wind chill factor is forty below as I talk to you. But despite the cold and snow, this city works and we finished our shooting schedule ahead of time. Chicago is the greatest." If the series holds up in the Nielsen ratings, Conrad will return in the spring to continue filming.

One of the unheralded accomplishments during Super Snow was the police work in reducing looting to a minimum. Usually during such a crisis, when the city resembles a ghost town, the looters are prevalent, breaking store windows to steal furs, TV sets, jewelry, etc. But Police Supt. Jim O'Grady took preventive measures by having mounted police and squad cars patrol the city's main shopping areas.

All together now, fellow frozen and snowbound Chicagoans—our new pledge of allegiance to the city includes: "Our weather, right or wrong!" . . . And who ever thought that our biggest growth industry would be snow removal?

Digging a car out along
South Boulevard in Oak Park.

(left) East winds make the walk east across Michigan Avenue at South Water almost unbearable. (below) Cars are completely buried by the snow on Crilly Court, near Eugenie.

Roger Simon
Mayor's idea people really dig snow

The Mayor's Office of Blocked Streets, Frozen Roads and Total Confusion has issued the following emergency bulletin:

Because the city's snow-removal efforts have been inadequate, the help of every citizen is needed. If Chicagoans will take the following steps, this city can be saved from disaster.

1. Eat snow. There are an estimated 3,099,391 people in Chicago, plus an additional 3,883,509 in the metropolitan area.

If every man, woman and child ate just seventeen pounds of snow, city streets would be clear by Easter.

The Mayor's Office of Snow Cookery has published a list of easy-to-prepare recipes for microwave, crockery-pot and deep-dish dining. Snow, combined with tomato sauce, a few cloves of garlic, white pepper and shallots, makes a tasty dish for home or office.

The Mayor's Office of Best Snow Recipe is offering a $5 award for the most original recipe using snow, sleet, ice or street salt as its main ingredient.

2. Mail snow to a friend. Even in the worst weather, the mail always goes through. Therefore, the Mayor's Office of Snow Mailing has advised residents that special delivery packages of snow are now being accepted.

All Chicagoans, especially those with friends in Houston, Oklahoma City, Los Angeles, Birmingham, New Orleans, Tampa and Little Rock, are urged to begin mailing snow immediately.

Twenty-gallon Hefty bags packed with snow and ice would cost only $87.50 to mail anywhere in the continental United States.

Imagine the delight of friends and relatives—many of whom have never seen it—at receiving genuine Chicago snow.

The mayor has offered to autograph all packages going to New York.

3. Pack. If heavy snows continue, the Mayor's Office of Head-'em-Up-and-Move-'em-Out will put Plan Bail-Out into effect.

This plan calls for all people whose last name begins with the letters A through M to move to Atlanta.

Those who last name begins with N through Z will move to Miami.

Residents of Bridgeport can remain where they are, since their streets are clear.

Residents are advised that they may bring personal effects with them, but are not allowed to bring Christmas trees, funny hats or anything made with garlic.

4. Pretend it's not there. The Mayor's Office of Putting One Over on the Public has advised residents that no snow has fallen on the city streets since 1967.

"We don't know what all the complaints are about," officials said. "Some people whine about every little thing. A few thousand people can't get to work; all traffic comes to a halt; supplies of bread, milk, heating oil and coal start to run out and pretty soon it's bitch, bitch, bitch.

"What's the big deal? What trees do they plant?"

5. Sit on it. Experts at the Mayor's Office of Sitting on It, estimate that if every city worker sat down on the snow, all snow and ice in Chicago would melt within twelve hours.

"No city workers can sit down on the job as well as our workers can," the mayor promised Tuesday.

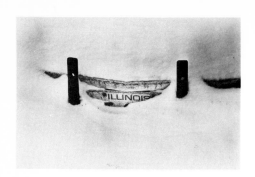

(above) Trudging across Wacker and South Water Streets. (right) Dump trucks put Chicago's snow back into the water system on the south side of the Chicago River between Clark and Dearborn.

Council gets Word

The City Council met Tuesday to talk about the snow crisis, and decided to blame it on God.

The alternative was to blame it on the mayor, and even though some aldermen have trouble distinguishing between the two, they picked God as the easier fall guy.

An elaborate four-color chart was brought in and propped up in the front of the Council chamber. The chart had squiggly lines and colored bars and measured daily snowfall, daily temperature and the wind chill factor. The chart looked like a bad day on Wall Street.

After a great deal of discussion, Alderman Roman Pucinski (41st) looked at the chart. He announced that there had been a lot of snow and that it was cold.

There was scattered applause.

Pucinski said that the snow was an act of nature and he blamed the weather forecasters for not knowing what God had up His sleeve.

He also said: "We have seen a great tragedy occur in this city. Some people suggest it is the greatest tragedy ever except for the Chicago Fire of 1871."

This may be true, but at least the Chicago Fire was warm.

To those who pointed out that thousands of motorists had stranded cars, side streets were blocked, public transportation is still not back to normal, and mountains of garbage are piling up, Pucinski said: "Nobody is perfect."

Alderman Edward Burke (14th) fired the opening salvo on the God-question by asking: "Can mere mortals take on nature?"

At least three aldermen thought that was what snowplows were for, but they were eventually voted down.

Burke contended that 1.3 million tons of snow already have been removed from city streets. Nobody asked how he knew, but one wag in the press corps suggested that some city worker was probably out there weighing it—at a nickel a ton.

"It is impossible to plan adequately for this kind of natural disaster," Burke said. "We are fighting with nature and the elements. The ebb and flow of governments has been changed by the weather."

It is unlikely that anything is going to ebb and flow in Chicago. In the first place, everything is still frozen. And in the second place, government doesn't ebb all that much around here.

The city administration has not lost a vote in the City Council in modern times. All fifty aldermen are Democrats, even though three of them call themselves independents. Generally speaking, in Chicago an independent is anyone who does not click his heels when the mayor enters the room.

The meeting Tuesday wasn't even supposed to take place, but the three independents got together and requested it. At the special meeting, Alderman Martin Oberman (43rd) wanted the Council to act as an investigative agency that would ask a whole bunch of embarrassing questions about why the snow didn't get picked up better.

For some reason, Mayor Bilandic did not like this idea. So he drew up his own resolution. That resolution called for a blue-ribbon panel to study things and report—by June 1.

By June 1, it is expected that snow will be less of a problem.

Mayor Bilandic was silent for the entire meeting, sometimes taking notes with a pencil as he rocked slowly in his chair. He rocked slowly when Oberman said: "We cannot afford to pass this idiotic resolution of the mayor's."

He rocked slowly when Alderman Ross Lathrop (5th) said: "This breakdown is not just a breakdown of city snow removal, but a breakdown of leadership."

The mayor rocked a little more happily when Alderman Bernard Stone (50th) did a long comparison of Chicago to the land of Oz and began his remarks by saying: "My fellow Munchkins, what if the yellow brick road had been packed with snow?"

In keeping with the religious theme of the meeting, Stone also said: "Men and equipment have limitations. What we get from God [the snow] has no limitations."

"In your scenario," Stone suggested to critics of the mayor, "the Wicked Witch of the West was the Almighty."

While everyone was wrestling with that, Alderman Edward Vrdolyak (10th) took the floor to lead an all-out attack on the independents. Many times during Vrdolyak's speech, Bilandic laughed and chuckled as he rocked.

The biggest laugh came when Vrdolyak told a story about how Mark Twain said if he met a dog on the road and fed him and cared for him, then the dog would never bite him.

"This is the thing that differentiates a dog from an independent alderman," Vrdolyak said.

Vrdolyak then apologized to the mayor for the nasty things the independents had said and concluded with the statement: "We support your leadership."

The Mayor won, 35-5, and everyone went home. But not before the city spirit was summed up by Eddie Burke.

"We understand the mood of the public and the nature of the public these days," he said. "Everyone is mad at everyone else.

"People are cursing and swearing at everyone else. That's human nature."

Naw, alderman, that's Chicago.

(left) Temporary delay on Menominee Street. (below) Firefighters put out the last touches of fire at American Paper Recycling on West Lake Street in Northlake.

116

Public Eye

"The Chicago Blizzard" is the newest drink at the Sheraton-Plaza here. You blend rum, cognac, Cointreau and lime juice with shaved ice. "It's slush with a real kick," said the hotel's general manager, David Semadeni. A good way to get plowed.

Leaping Blizzards! The big Wednesday sign on the easel inside the Conrad Hilton Hotel read: "Mayor Bilandic's Quality of Life Conference Postponed Until February."

Chicago's terrible winter makes Finland's energy secretary "feel like home." Erkki Vaara, who's here for a symposium, said, "Today we could have exactly the same weather in Helsinki." (Vaara also thinks Chicago has more severe winters than southern Finland, where most Finns live.) You getting a Helsinking feeling?

The snow-packed roof caved in at Dunbrook Shopping Plaza, Northbrook, triggering a blaze that razed four businesses. They include Shear Elegance beauty salon and Dunbrook Pharmacy. "There go my prescriptions, up in smoke," mourned a customer named Alice. Too bad about the drugstore, said a pal. "I had prescriptions there, of course," said Alice, "but the *important* prescriptions were for my hair, at the beauty shop."

Famed Chicagoans revealed their sniffle-fighting secrets to a Blue Cross-Blue Shield Cold Clinic:

—Artis Gilmore of the Bulls: "I drink loads of tea and honey, and then I ignore it."

—Lee Phillip of Channel 2: "I take six Vitamin C tablets a day instead of the usual three, and go on a liquid diet. Plenty of hot water and lemon juice. It clears out the baddies."

—Restaurateur Gene Sage: "I get mean and miserable. Then I drink good cognac. Then I don't care if I'm mean and miserable."

—Kup the columnist: "I totally ignore it."

—Down in Springfield, Secretary of State Alan Dixon said, "I usually get it in the throat. So I rest my voice. That's very difficult for a public official."

The De Kalb Daily Chronicle asked readers to name our hideous Illinois winter. The winning entry is "The Incredible Bulk" (which also was a recent Sun-Times headline). The 300 other printable suggestions included:

—The Blizzard of Odds.
—Snow Wars.
—Supercalifragilisticexpialidocioussnowslush.
—Killinois.
—Super Dump.
—The Year of the Blankity Blanket.
—Baby Makin' Time of '79.

Bozo's Circus was canceled Wednesday for perhaps the third time in its seventeen-year history. A tape of the January 8 Bozo's Circus was shown instead. "Inclement weather" was the reason given for the cancellation by Al Hall, the show's producer. "Neither Bozo nor Cookie can get in because of the snow," said Hall. "Same goes for one of the musicians." The popular, live noon-hour kids' show originates in Channel 9's studios at 2501 W. Bradley Pl. Wednesday's ticket-holders, who wrote in for ducats eight years ago, will be invited to other shows this year.

True Chicago weather story. He spent hours digging out his car, parked in front of his home on the Northwest Side. Then he drove to the store for some food. When he returned home, a stranger was starting to park in his space! The stranger refused to move! The stranger parked and locked his car, and walked away! So our guy got his shovel, and shoveled all the snow back onto the stranger's car. Then our guy hooked up his garden hose to a nonfrozen faucet, and sprayed the snow until the stranger's car was encased in Chicago's biggest ice cube.

Mayor Bilandic and mom Minnie may be responsible for Chicago's Thursday sun. "I've been praying" for the snow to stop, Bilandic told City Hall newsmen Wednesday. "And I've asked everyone else to pray. I'm going to visit my saintly old mother today, and I'm going to put her on the case." Who's the patron saint of clear skies?

There's money in Chicago snowstorms. Several youngsters have been selling "Blizzard of '79" T-shirts near the Michigan Av. bridge. The cost: $5 each. Get yours, then ask Mayor Bilandic for your Distinguished Snow Medal with CTA battle stars.

Actor John Travolta and his manager got stuck in deep snow, just like the rest of us. Their car was finally pulled from the Wyoming drifts by Mike and Gerri Schneider's four-wheel-drive vehicle. The Schneiders were "very excited" after realizing they'd rescued Travolta. Grateful Travolta responded with Saturday night fervor: He treated the Schneiders to a steak dinner, cooked by his manager at a mountain cabin. Travolta had been skiing incognito at Jackson Hole (he wore a face mask on the slopes).

They're telling Chicago jokes in Cleveland, says Larry Green. He's Midwest bureau chief for the L.A. Times, based in Chicago. Larry reports Cleveland's top Chicago gag is:

—Q. "What happened to winter this year?"
—A. "It all got dumped on Chicago."

Ha-ha. We spent a month in Cleveland one weekend.

Puns & Fun. "I saw Eddie Gold salt the banana he was eating," says Dave Manthey. "He didn't want anyone to slip on the peel." . . . "There's no business like snow business." (Ed Malinowski). . . . "Chicago's snow

(above) Protecting a cleared parking spot in the 2500 block of North Lakeview. (left) An early morning pedestrian fights the cold and snow at Wacker and Michigan. (right) Victim of the storm found at 1150 North State.

cleanup story would make a good movie," says Fred Rosen. "They could call it 'The Invasion of the Caterpillars.'"

First Chicagoan: "The blizzard of '79 wouldn't have been mishandled if Mayor Daley were alive." Second Chicagoan: "It wouldn't have been mishandled if Mayor Bilandic were alive."

"I feel like a baseball player," says Fred Rosen. "I'm touching all bases while sliding home." . . . Joe Cummings has a new word: "Glice." It's glassy ice. . . . "This snow is making people flaky" (Charles Markman).

Sun-Timesman Herb Gould, whose pen name is Jackson Park Alstops III, wrote a punny poem titled "An L of A Fix." Here's part of it:

It was a Howard ride from the North Side.
The Ls were Fullerton; they could hold no Morse.
And on every platform could be heard this chor's:
'Brrr. Win. Let me in.'
But it was Granville room only.

Fighting the elements at Wacker and South Water Streets.

After the Storm

It was magnificent and malevolent, awesome and infuriating. It was white and deep and the devil to move. It broke records and collapsed roofs, closed schools and caused deaths. It inspired heroism and unselfishness, pettiness and exploitation, humor and surrender.

It buried cars, stranded travelers, reduced crime, strained patience, paralyzed traffic, canceled culture, hurt business and harried politicians. It shut down the world's busiest airport, it fouled up the CTA, it made walking a distasteful adventure. It exhausted snow-removal crews, police officers and firefighters, who sacrificed sleep for service. Getting to and from work became a long day's journey into night.

It was enormously expensive. It made the founders of Chicago look incredibly stupid for locating a city where they did. It will leave scars on all of us. The perverse pride that Chicagoans develop in the inhumanly horrible winter weather they endure—a kind of defense mechanism—would have a fresh atrocity to bemoan and gloat over. But it would have been better if it had never happened.

It was the Blizzard of '79. Try to forget it.

—Paul Galloway

I Survived

Credits

Photography:
Don Bierman, 17, 18, 39, 59; Bob Black, 66, 69;
James DePree, cover, 30, 49, 54-55, 56, 58, 65, 70, 74, 77, 78, 86, 112;
Richard Derk, 33, 47, 60, 85, 86, 87, 110, 116;
Jim Frost, 32, 37, 40, 41, 47, 63, 64, 101;
Keith Hale, 3, 79, 90, 93, 98, 118; Martha Hartnett, 60;
Kevin Horan, 18, 22, 24, 27, 29, 34, 45, 53, 54, 73, 79, 91, 96, 100, 102, 108;
Charles Kirman, 88; James Klepitsch, 28, 30, 31, 36, 41, 43, 44, 67, 95;
Bob Langer, 57; R. B. Leffingwell, 76, 116;
Jack Lenahan, 42, 45, 65, 89, 92, 96, 104, 106;
Jim Mescall, 27, 61, 62; Gene Pesek, 28, 36, 51, 63, 88;
Carmen Reporto, 34, 48; Perry C. Riddle, 114;
Jerry Tomaselli, 20, 21, 26, 35, 48-49, 50, 51, 52, 53, 68, 69, 75,
77, 80, 81, 82, 87, 91, 97, 112, 114, 118, 119, 120;
John H. White, 26, 114.

Illustration: Mike Lancaster, 18
Cover design: Bill Linden
Book design: Steve Miller/Features Press

5835